Identifying
&
Serving

Culturally and Linguistically
Diverse Gifted Students

Identifying & Serving

Culturally and Linguistically Diverse Gifted Students

Lezley Collier Lewis, Ph.D.,
Annie Rivera, &
Debbie Roby

PRUFROCK PRESS INC.
WACO, TEXAS

Dedication

For all of the support of my friends and family who gave me the "gift" of time and space to think, learn, create, and dream—I appreciate and love each of you beyond measure. But most of all, the White Tigers, who for 2 years sat around the kitchen table and put words to dreams and made the vision a reality.

—Lezley

For my loving husband, Gonzalo, and Cami, who have been supportive and patient with me through this endeavor, and Greg and Theresa Jeong, who gave me the best education possible—because of the Lord's blessings and all of you, I am "gifted."

—Annie

For those over time and distance who have nurtured my "gifts" through professional trust and collaboration, and for my husband and sons who have provided me strength, support, and the freedom to be me.

—Debbie

Library of Congress Cataloging-in-Publication Data

Lewis, Lezley Collier, 1962-
  Identifying and serving culturally and linguistically diverse gifted students / by Lezley Collier Lewis,
Annie Rivera, and Debbie Roby.
      p. cm.
  Includes bibliographical references.
  ISBN 978-1-59363-844-3 (pbk.)
  1. Gifted children--Education--United States. 2. Children of minorities--Education--United States. 3.
Linguistic minorities--Education--United States. I. Rivera, Annie, 1978- II. Roby, Debbie, 1970- III.
Title.
  LC3993.9.L49 2012
  371.95--dc23
                              2011038638

Copyright ©2012 Prufrock Press, Inc.

Edited by Jennifer Robins

Cover and layout design by Raquel Trevino

ISBN-13: 978-1-59363-844-3

At the time of this book's publication, all facts and figures cited are the most current available; all telephone numbers, addresses, and website URLs are accurate and active; all publications, organizations,
websites, and other resources exist as described in this book; and all have been verified. The authors
and Prufrock Press make no warranty or guarantee concerning the information and materials given
out by organizations or content found at the websites, and we are not responsible for any changes that
occur after this book's publication. If you find an error or believe that a resource listed here is not as
described, please contact Prufrock Press.

Prufrock Press Inc.
P.O. Box 8813
Waco, TX 76714-8813
Phone: (800) 998-2208
Fax: (800) 240-0333
http://www.prufrock.com

Table of Contents

Introduction

We are not in a position in which we have nothing to work with. We already have capacities, talents, direction, missions, callings.

—Abraham Maslow

Identifying and Serving Culturally and Linguistically Diverse Gifted Students is a tangible representation of the professional collaboration that we value. Throughout our careers, each of us has sought like-minded colleagues who put students and their best interests at the forefront of daily professional efforts. Each of us has spent, and continues to spend, countless hours advocating for the use of best practice philosophies and instructional practices that are tailored to serve students' educational needs. As we literally brought our like minds, our passion for education, and our professional experiences to the table, we discovered that this book needed to be written.

As district-level program supervisors of bilingual and gifted education programs, we worked in isolation within our programs, serving our respective student populations. No extensive or relevant professional dialogue existed between the two programs—only compliance with traditional bilingual, English as a second language (ESL), and gifted education service models. There was inconsistency between programming coupled with a lack of coordination that served to perpetuate inequity for our culturally and linguistically diverse (CLD) gifted students. As critical conversations occurred around scheduling and services, we realized how much more effective our services could be if our efforts were combined, focusing on the students and their needs instead of the individual work we were doing in our respective programs. The idea that we could shift from managing compliance and isolated learning to focusing on the students' potential and needs became the momentum behind our work. Although unintended, the lack of a plan to provide integrated services to gifted CLD students clearly limited our effectiveness.

As our bilingual, ESL, and gifted student population continued to overlap, we sought each other's professional knowledge about programming services and student learning. The realization that we could come together around the student, across program service lines, to integrate and form a coordinated approach for supporting teachers and identifying and serving students was the epiphany for this book's content. But first, we had to learn and understand the core knowledge supporting each other's work in our respective areas.

This book is comprised of eight chapters, organized into three distinct sections. The first section, Foundational Principles Composing the Education of the Gifted CLD Learner, introduces the reader to the gifted and culturally and linguistically diverse student. Basic theories and tenets regarding the fields of second language acquisition and gifted and talented education are affirmed in the first two chapters, creating a common understanding about gifted CLD learners. We have identified what we believe to be the critical components of bilingual, ESL, and gifted education in Chapters 1 and 2.

Chapters 3 and 4 comprise the second section, Examining Existing Programmatic Structures. This section equips the reader to consider the programs that are already offered within the school or district through a novel perspective. Examining existing programs through an inventory-style checklist is inadequate; rather, educators must assess how culturally and linguistically responsive those programs are in meeting the needs of gifted CLD students. Chapter 3 sets forth a system for identifying inherent system inequities as well as a new way for thinking about giftedness. We have seen the positive impact of such professional engagement at all levels of education. Chapter 4 shares a new model for blending specialized programming in schools with the Program Design Wheel. On campuses, we find that schools achieve more when administrators embrace the collaboration of special services, and teachers receive much-deserved support when innovating instructional practices to meet the demands of differentiation.

The final section, Service Delivery, encompasses Chapters 5–8. These chapters discuss how to effectively deliver instruction for the gifted CLD student through pedagogical techniques and methodology, program collaboration, professional preparation, family and community involvement, and program evaluation. Chapter 5 focuses on the aspects of curriculum and instruction in a diverse differentiated classroom. Chapter 6 provides an instrument called the 4P Framework, which is used for coordinating planning and embedding professional development. As district program models become increasingly sophisticated, parents and communities in which these programs exist must be partnered in the development. Chapter 7 demonstrates how to partner through conversation starters and guidelines in order to better identify and serve gifted CLD students. Chapter 8 offers a rubric for evaluating the components of a gifted education program that serves a culturally and linguistically diverse student population. In addition, it ties together all of the main concepts presented in the other chapters.

The intended audience for this book is all encompassing. Written with educators, campus and district administrators, and program developers in mind, this book will positively transform the educational system for working with gifted CLD student populations. Individuals with little to no experience working with gifted CLD students will gain a thorough understanding of the foundations of gifted education and the needs of CLD learners. Individuals with considerable experience serving gifted CLD students will benefit from the original methods presented for gauging how well this population of learners is being served and improving programs efficiently and effectively.

Maslow's belief that "We are not in a position in which we have nothing to work with" sums up the premise of this book: Everything that we need to know as educators, we know. Everything that we intrinsically need to serve students, we have. As Maslow eloquently continued, "We already have capacities, talents, direction, missions, callings." It is the position of this book's authors that as a profession, educators have more extensive knowledge and resources than ever before to be effective in teaching. If this is the case, then why aren't all students reaching their potential? Why aren't the capacities, talents, direction, missions, and callings enough? There must be a repurposing of the work, a rethinking of how these qualities are applied in the context of education. The rethinking must occur in order to better serve the needs of 21st-century students.

Rapid demographic shifts, patterns of immigration, and increasing disparity in socioeconomic status are changing schools at a pace that educators cannot match and struggle to understand. The current environment demands that educators bring students up to speed and cover all required material in too little time. Educators from across the nation are feeling the pressure to do more with less, to overcome what appear to be insurmountable barriers, and to do the impossible every day. As educators, we empathize with the frustration. We understand the ever-changing dynamics of the classroom, and more importantly, have been witness to the changing demographics of the student population.

We organized the book's information around the understanding that educators will read it for a variety of purposes: to learn more about working with gifted CLD students, to address program deficiencies centered on CLD students and gifted services, and to review the effectiveness of existing gifted services. The information in the book is organized in a consistent and predictable manner: Each chapter has a purpose presented in the beginning and a preview of terms and the applicable *NAGC Pre-K–Grade 12 Gifted Programming Standards* (National Association for Gifted Children [NAGC], 2010) to assist the reader in understanding what's covered in the chapter. Throughout the book, the term *gifted education* will be used to refer to the encompassing category of gifted *and* talented, unless otherwise stated. The use of the educational phrase gifted education is for the reader's ease in following the text.

> Just think of something that would be "wonderful" if it were only "possible." Then set out to make it possible.
>
> —Armand Hammer

As authors, we envisioned many "wonderful somethings" that, if they were possible, would change the course of gifted education and services for culturally and linguistically diverse children. We set out to do that which is possible—to present the vision of these wonderful things to other educators who are vested in the education of gifted CLD students.

Section I:

Foundational Principles Composing the Education of the Gifted CLD Learner

Chapter 1

Second Language Acquisition

The purpose of Chapter 1 is to construct a framework for understanding the principles of second language acquisition.

Preview of Standard(s)/Term(s):

- ➦ *NAGC Standard 6: Professional Development: 6.1.1*: Educators systematically participate in ongoing, research-supported professional development that addresses the foundations of gifted education, characteristics of students with gifts and talents, assessment, curriculum planning and instruction, learning environments, and programming.
- ➦ *NAGC Standard 6: Professional Development: 6.4.1*: Educators respond to cultural and personal frames of reference when teaching students with gifts and talents.
- ➦ *Linguistic accommodation*: Adjustments made in order to achieve academic instruction commensurate to the language proficiency level of the student.
- ➦ *Holophrastic*: One-word communication that encompasses a complete understanding or meaning. For example, toddlers may say "milk" or "ouch" to express their needs.
- ➦ *Telegraphic*: One- or two-word phrases that communicate complete understanding or meanings. For example, toddlers may say "me cookie" or "toy mine."
- ➦ *L1*: Abbreviation for one's native language.

→ *L2*: Abbreviation for one's target language.

→ *Metalinguistic*: One's awareness of one's own language.

→ *i + 1*: Symbolic representation for comprehensible input. Input that is comprehensible plus one level of language above one's current language ability.

→ *Cognates*: Words that have the same or similar meanings and spellings in another language. For example, "carro" in Spanish means the same as "car" in English. (Note that there are also false cognates, in which two words may look similar in two languages but do not have the same meaning. For example, "embarazada," which means "pregnant" in Spanish, looks similar to "embarrassed" in English.)

→ *Language objectives*: Articulated knowledge or skills that students are taught and/or required to master as part of their core language instruction. Language objectives explicitly address one or more of the four domains of language.

→ *Image streaming*: An activity that requires uninterrupted, verbal descriptions that utilize visualization and articulation of images. Image streaming encourages vocabulary development and the use of all senses to describe visualizations.

→ *Realia*: Any tangible object that is used for instructional purposes. For example, using an actual plant to demonstrate when teaching about the parts of a plant.

→ *Majority language*: The language spoken and used for communication by the mainstream majority; the common vernacular of society.

→ *Minority language*: The language spoken by the population not in the mainstream majority; not recognized as the common vernacular of mainstream society.

Foundational Principles of
Second Language Acquisition

Constructing a framework for understanding the principles of second language acquisition is the goal of this chapter. Although the principles provided are not mutually exclusive and only touch on the broad scope of work done in the field of second language acquisition, they provide the basic understanding the classroom teacher needs in order to meet the needs of a diverse group of learners.

The challenge of education grows increasingly dense and diverse as time progresses. Classroom composition has changed dramatically in recent decades, yet curriculum and instruction lag behind as the demands on the classroom teacher increase. "Today, more kinds of children come to school and stay in school, bringing with them a greater range of backgrounds and needs" (Tomlinson, 1999, p. 20). The pressure on the teacher to be proficient in all aspects of specialized services is overwhelming.

Working with English language learners (ELLs) is especially challenging, as the classroom teacher must be competent in the second language acquisition principles that guide understanding and best support instructional practices for ELLs. The teacher's skill set is further complicated by the need to identify and provide services to ELLs who exhibit giftedness. Tomlinson (1999) noted, "All children are entitled to teachers who will do everything in their power to help them realize their potential every day" (p. 21). If an English language learner is gifted and never served appropriately, the child's ability to reach his or her gifted potential diminishes.

> Teacher competency requires:
> ✔ working knowledge of second language acquisition principles and
> ✔ appropriately defining giftedness in ELLs.

In order to build teacher competence, nine foundational principles of second language acquisition have been identified and are shared below. A working knowledge of the principles provides the groundwork for educators working with culturally and linguistically diverse students.

Principle 1: Domains of Language

There are four domains of language: listening, speaking, reading, and writing. Listening and reading are often referred to as the receptive domains because both require receiving language and processing the meaning of what is being spoken or written. Speaking and writing are referred to as the expressive or productive domains. As the terms suggest, speaking and writing require the production of language in either the spoken or written form. It is important to note that the second language learner can vary in proficiency in each of these four domains. For a child learning a new language, the receptive processes (listening and reading) may come more quickly, whereas the productive processes (writing and especially speaking) may come later (Vogt & Echevarria, 2008). Although the receptive and productive domains may appear at different times, each must be supported with linguistically accommodated instruction. Effective teachers make linguistic accommodations to meet the needs of students in all four domains and also create opportunities for students to prac-

Table 1.1

Principle 1: Domains of Language

Researcher(s)	Finding(s)	Classroom Application(s)
Vogt and Echevarria (2008)	<ul><li>There are four domains of language: reading, writing, speaking, and listening.</li><li>The receptive domains include listening and reading.</li><li>The productive domains include writing and speaking.</li></ul>	<ul><li>Teachers should be aware that the four domains are interrelated, but the productive domains may present themselves later than the receptive domains.</li></ul>

tice both the receptive and productive domains through purposeful activities. Table 1.1 highlights this principle.

Principle 2: Stages of Second Language Acquisition

Teachers who work with second language learners must understand the stages of language acquisition. According to Krashen and Terrell's (1983) natural approach theory, there are five stages: pre-production, early production, speech emergence, intermediate fluency, and advanced fluency. Students who are in the pre-production stage of learning a language have minimal comprehension and have not yet produced speech or writing. For this reason, the pre-production stage is also referred to as the silent period. During the preproduction stage, students should never be forced to produce language. Although it may seem that there is no progression, students are honing their receptive skills, which in turn will positively affect their productive skills in due time. In the early production stage, ELLs start to produce language. Their receptive and productive domains are still limited, but they can speak and write in holophrastic strings.

In the speech emergence stage, students acquiring a second language are able to produce telegraphic speech and writing. Although students in this stage still make grammatical errors, their comprehension is more advanced than in previous stages. Those in the intermediate fluency and advanced fluency stages exhibit full receptive and productive skills. However, students in the intermediate fluency stage make grammatical errors, while those in the advanced fluency stage demonstrate fluency comparable to their native English-speaking peers. It is essential that teachers working with English language learners know the stage at which their students find themselves. Although students should never be forced out of their stage, teachers can facilitate the acceleration of each of the phases by utilizing stage-appropriate questioning strategies, sentence stems, and teacher prompts. Table 1.2 highlights this principle.

Table 1.2
Principle 2: Stages of Second Language Acquisition

Researcher(s)	Finding(s)	Classroom Application(s)
Krashen and Terrell (1983)	▪ There are five stages of language acquisition: pre-production, early production, speech emergence, intermediate fluency, and advanced fluency.	▪ Teachers must recognize the stage of language acquisition that the student is experiencing and be patient with language acquisition. ▪ Teachers should be respectful of the stage the student is experiencing and orchestrate learning around stage progression. ▪ Teachers should understand that even though a student is in the pre-production stage, it is not an indicator of the student's learning or absence of learning.

Principle 3: Basic Interpersonal Communication Skills and Cognitive Academic Language Proficiency

There are two distinct types of language proficiency: Basic Interpersonal Communication Skills (BICS) and Cognitive Academic Language Proficiency (CALP). Coined by Canadian linguist Jim Cummins in 1979, BICS and CALP refer to social language proficiency and academic language proficiency, respectively. According to Cummins, it takes approximately 1–2 years from initial exposure to achieve proficiency in BICS and from 5–7 years to acquire proficiency in CALP. These points can be visualized using Cummins's iceberg metaphor (see Figure 1.1). The tip of the iceberg, which can be seen above the surface of the water, corresponds to social language, or BICS. BICS proficiency is demonstrated in everyday communication and is acquired through social contexts. Teachers often refer to it as "playground" language. Below the surface of the water lies CALP. This language is not easily seen, as it is "hidden" below the water, yet is essential to express academic understanding and achievement. CALP requires a longer amount of time to achieve because academic language is more abstract and thus provides fewer contexts than BICS.

Teachers of English language learners who have a clear understanding of BICS versus CALP recognize that BICS fluency is not equivalent to overall English fluency. Many second language learners are fully capable of expressing themselves in social contexts, yet have difficulty with academic tasks in the target language. Using the same line of reasoning, such difficulty may not necessarily be due to a lack of academic ability; the ELL may not have CALP to demonstrate understanding in L2. Table 1.3 highlights this principle.

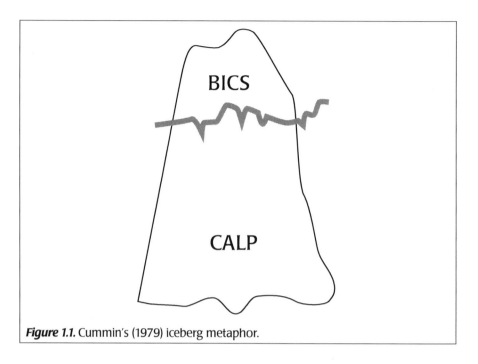

Figure 1.1. Cummin's (1979) iceberg metaphor.

Table 1.3

Principle 3: Basic Interpersonal Communication Skills
and Cognitive Academic Language Proficiency

Researcher(s)	Finding(s)	Classroom Application(s)
Cummins (1979)	▪ There are two distinct types of language proficiency: Basic Interpersonal Communication Skills (BICS) and Cognitive Academic Language Proficiency (CALP).	▪ Teachers should not be misled when students are effectively communicating in the social context; this does not mean that a student's academic language proficiency is on the same level as his or her social language proficiency. ▪ A student's performance as evidenced by BICS should not be an indicator of his or her CALP.

Principle 4: Context-Embedded/Context-Reduced Language and Cognitively Demanding/Undemanding Tasks

Context plays a crucial role in the acquisition of language. As described in Principle 3, English language learners tend to acquire BICS more rapidly than CALP because of the richness of context in social language. According to Cummins (1981), students are able to acquire BICS through gestures, high-level contact with peers, the expression and tone of the speaker, and contextual cues within the environment. CALP is more abstract, requires a higher level of literacy due to the expository nature of academic language, and is accompanied

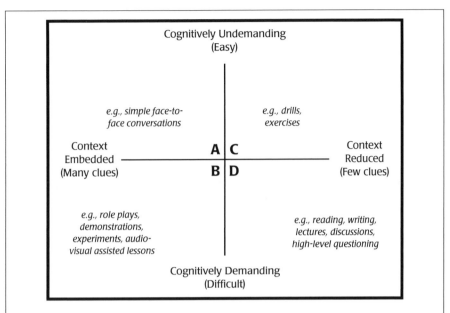

Figure 1.2. Cummins's (1981) context-embedded versus context-reduced model.

by fewer nonverbal cues. Academic tasks tend to be more cognitively demanding whereas social activities tend to be less demanding. Cummins (1981) asserted that the distinction between cognitively demanding and cognitively undemanding tasks is further differentiated by the amount of context provided (see Figure 1.2).

For example, although a social conversation using BICS is cognitively undemanding, it can be highly context-embedded if the conversation takes place in person rather than over the telephone, which is context-reduced. A science lesson using all CALP is cognitively demanding, but if students are involved in a hands-on science experiment with rich visual cues, the lesson is much more context-embedded than a reading assignment from a scientific journal about the same concepts.

Teachers of ELLs should always be aware of how much context students have to use, especially with cognitively demanding tasks. Providing purposeful visual cues, gestures, and expressions to deliver instruction that requires a high level of academic language will situate the students in a successful learning environment. Table 1.4 highlights this principle.

Principle 5: Input Hypothesis

In 1982, researcher Stephen Krashen published a theory of second language acquisition. The theory is comprised of five hypotheses that serve to bet-

Table 1.4
Principle 4: Context-Embedded/Context-Reduced Language
and Cognitively Demanding/Undemanding Tasks

Researcher(s)	Finding(s)	Classroom Application(s)
Cummins (1981)	• Activities/tasks can be categorized as cognitively demanding/undemanding. • A continuum demonstrating the range of the context richness varies from context embedded to context reduced.	• Teachers should provide as much context as possible when teaching cognitively demanding material.

ter instruct educators working with second language learners: the acquisition-learning hypothesis, the monitor hypothesis, the natural order hypothesis, the input hypothesis, and the affective filter hypothesis. The input hypothesis provides a foundation for gauging instruction for second language learners.

The input hypothesis elaborates several fundamental principles that inform the process of language acquisition. *Comprehensible input* (i.e., level i + 1) represents language structures that are a little beyond an individual's current level of language competence (i.e., level i). These are made comprehensible through the use of context, background knowledge, and environmental cues. This application of comprehensible input is successful when an individual acquires the structures of the language through the development of meaning. Krashen (1982) maintained that substantial and successful communication supports level i + 1 and language will naturally emerge as a result. The speaking fluency involved in language acquisition is not explicitly taught, but rather emerges as a result of the natural exposure to and comprehension of the second language. Table 1.5 highlights this principle.

Principle 6: Affective Filter Hypothesis

As mentioned above, another hypothesis in the Krashen (1982) theory of second language acquisition is the affective filter hypothesis, which extends the input hypothesis and addresses the impact of affective conditions on a learner's ability to acquire a second language. Affective conditions include student self-esteem and confidence, motivation, and anxiety levels. The classroom environment is one factor that affects these conditions.

The affective filter hypothesis establishes the importance of students' belief in their ability to acquire—and their motivation to learn—a second language, as well as the tremendous effect of the classroom on these affective conditions. A motivated second language learner succeeds in a classroom where the subject content is tied to context and made comprehensible—and where the environment is free of anxiety and fear of error. Second language learners should

Table 1.5
Principle 5: Input Hypothesis

Researcher	Finding(s)	Classroom Application(s)
Krashen (1982)	• Krashen's theory of second language acquisition is comprised of five hypotheses established to support the natural acquisition of language. • The input hypothesis establishes comprehensible input (level i + 1), instructs the learner's ability to make meaning out of language, and addresses the emergence of speaking fluency.	• Teachers should teach at level i + 1—using no "dumbed-down" language. • Teachers should understand the importance of a print, discourse, and language-enriched environment. Learning is purposeful, relevant, and interesting.

Table 1.6
Principle 6: Affective Filter Hypothesis

Researcher(s)	Finding(s)	Classroom Application(s)
Krashen (1982)	• Krashen's theory of second language acquisition is comprised of five hypotheses established to support the natural acquisition of language. • The affective filter hypothesis focuses on the affective conditions in a classroom. Minimal error correction is present, and speaking in the second language is never forced.	• Students with high motivation and less anxiety are better equipped for second language acquisition. • The classroom environment should be one of low stress and high student engagement and motivation. • Error correction is achieved through modeling of correct language structures. • Differentiated ways for communication exist in the classroom; speaking is never forced outside of language proficiency stage.

have the opportunity to dialogue with native target language peers to allow the second language to emerge naturally. Table 1.6 highlights this principle.

Principle 7: Language Transfer Theory

According to Isurin (2005), "Transfer is a traditional term from psychology of learning which means imposition of previously learned patterns onto a new learning situation" (p. 1115). One instance of this is Cross Linguistic Influence (CLI), which occurs when an individual's first language (L1) interacts in some way with his or her acquisition of a second language (L2). The child can transfer the cognitive skills, language structure, and system of meaning he already possesses in his own language to a new language (Vygotsky, 1962), and a metalinguistic knowledge of the organizational principles of language can facilitate this transfer (Cohen, McAlister, Rolstad, & MacSwan, 2005).

There are two types of language transfer in CLI: positive and negative. Positive transfer (facilitation) occurs when the two language systems' structures align well with each other, easing transition. An example of positive transfer is a cognate. Negative transfer (inhibition) exists when the structure and meaning of two language systems do not match well, such that a second language learner cannot draw upon one system to transition to the other. The ability to quickly acquire a second language system can be predicted by the ease of transfer. In second language acquisition, the knowledge of the native language (L1) can indeed facilitate or inhibit the learner's progress in mastering a new language (L2; Isurin, 2005).

In addition to CLI, a student's knowledge of the structures that comprise his or her native language are enhanced by the acquisition of the second language. "The child learns to see his language as one particular system among many, to view its phenomena under more general categories, and this leads to awareness of his linguistic operations" (Vygotsky, 1962, p. 110). Table 1.7 highlights this principle.

Principle 8: Contexts of Second Language Acquisition

There are two contexts of second language acquisition: simultaneous and sequential. In simultaneous second language acquisition, a student learns the second language at the same time that he or she acquires the first. Sequential second language acquisition occurs when the second language is learned after the first has been established. For sequential second language learners, the process of language acquisition is not what language is but rather what *this* (the second) language is (Tabors, 2008). For sequential second language learners, the process of language acquisition is focused on acquiring vocabulary to attach to existing cognitive structures rather than acquiring cognitive structures simultaneously with language. This is the quintessential difference between learning language as content versus learning content through language. Regardless of the type and timing of the second language acquisition, the first language plays an important role. The level of children's mother tongue is a strong predictor of their second language development (Cummins, n.d., para. 12). Table 1.8 highlights this principle.

Principle 9: Sociocultural Component of Learning

In their chapter, "Predicting Second Language Academic Success in English Using the Prism Model," Collier and Thomas (2007) discussed the components necessary for a holistic approach to educating the second language learner through the Prism Model (see Figure 1.3). The Prism Model is comprised of

Table 1.7
Principle 7: Language Transfer Theory

Researcher(s)	Finding(s)	Classroom Application(s)
Isurin (2005)	▪ L1 has an effect on the acquisition of L2. ▪ There are two types of language transfer: positive (facilitation) and negative (inhibition).	▪ Teachers need to know the structure of the language systems in order to facilitate positive transfer and address negative transfer. ▪ Teachers need to know that negative transfer between two language systems by the student is not always indicative of a language disability.

Table 1.8
Principle 8: Contexts of Second Language Acquisition

Researcher(s)	Finding(s)	Classroom Application(s)
Tabors (2008)	▪ There are two contexts of second language acquisition: simultaneous and sequential. ▪ The level of L1 is a strong predictor of L2 development.	▪ Teachers need to understand each student's type of language acquisition. ▪ If errors are presented based on the type of language acquisition, it is not indicative of cognitive failure on the student's part. ▪ If a student is a sequential second language learner, the foundation for a language system is already in place. ▪ If a student is a simultaneous second language learner, the structures are still emerging and will require a different level of differentiation when transfer is involved. ▪ Teachers need to understand the importance of L1 in a student's acquisition of L2.

four components: sociocultural, linguistic, academic, and cognitive processes. These four components (each addressing the first and second language) influence the success of a second language learner in school and must be present and in sync for the learner to experience optimal success. At the center of the Prism Model is the student, whose ability to organize, acculturate, and communicate is the key to his or her survival.

> It is crucial that educators provide a socioculturally supportive school environment for language minority students that allows natural language, academic, and cognitive development to flourish in both L1 and L2, comparable to the sociocultural support for ongoing language, academic, and cognitive development that native English speakers are provided in school. (Thomas & Collier, 2001, p. 324)

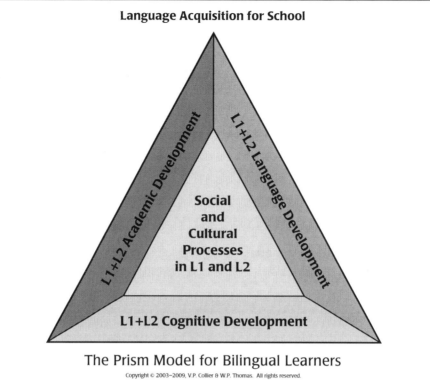

Figure 1.3. Collier and Thomas's (2009) Prism Model. From *Educating English Learners for a Transformed World* (p. 34), by V. P. Collier and W. P. Thomas, 2009, Albuquerque, NM: Fuente Press. Reprinted with permission of authors.

For the second language learner, a school environment where culture and language are valued in the school and classroom is critical. Table 1.9 highlights this principle.

Conclusion

The foundational second language acquisition principles do not function in isolation, but rather work in conjunction, overlapping in purpose and execution. Principles 1–3 focus on the learner, Principles 4–6 focus on the teacher, Principles 7–8 focus on specificity of language acquisition and the teacher's role, and Principle 9 synthesizes all principles, providing the larger context for the application of the linguistics, academic, and social aspects. Figure 1.4 offers a visual representation of how the principles overlap.

To further assist educators in applying the foundation principles to classroom practice, Table 1.10 provides a visual representation that begins with research and continues through to classroom application.

Table 1.9
Principle 9: Sociocultural Component of Learning

Researcher(s)	Finding(s)	Classroom Application(s)
Collier and Thomas (2009)	▪ The Prism Model identifies four components (language development, cognitive development, academic development, and social and cultural processes) necessary for a holistic approach to educating the second language learner.	▪ Teachers need to know the four components of the Prism Model, which are intricately linked to one another.

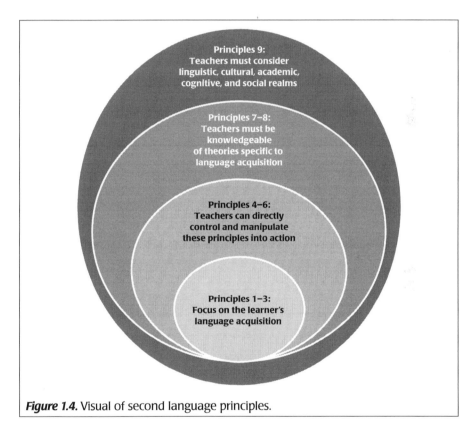

Figure 1.4. Visual of second language principles.

Once the classroom teacher is familiar with the principles of second language acquisition, he or she will be able to recognize and identify gifted behaviors in a manner that is not tied to language. For example, students who are not verbal because they are in their silent period of language acquisition may manifest gifted behavior through other means of communication. The key to identifying gifted behaviors in culturally and linguistically diverse students is to understand the perspective of the student in a language-neutral context. Chapter 2 will discuss giftedness and CLD students.

Table 1.10
Second Language Principles

Principle	Finding(s)	Classroom Application	Instructional Strategies	Examples of Instructional Strategies
Principle 1: Domains of Language	▪ There are four domains of language: reading, writing, speaking, and listening. ▪ The receptive domains include listening and reading. ▪ The productive domains include writing and speaking.	▪ Teachers should be aware that domains are interrelated, but the productive domains may present later than the receptive domains.	▪ Teachers should incorporate listening, reading, writing, and student discourse activities. ▪ These activities should be framed in a classroom objective. These objectives are structured around student learning and are visible to the students in the classroom (e.g., written on the board). ▪ Objectives should follow sheltered English instruction models.	▪ Teachers should include: ¤ listening-based activities (e.g., media, technology associated with listening, Inside-Outside Circle [Kagan, 1994]).; ¤ structured reading activities (e.g., Guided Reading [Fountas & Pinnell, 1996], partner reading, choral reading, echo reading); ¤ writing-based activities (e.g., responding to text through illustration, developmentally appropriate writing activities, journal writing); and ¤ student speaking activities (e.g., conversation prompts, think alouds, image streaming [Wenger & Poe, 1996], demonstrations, modeling, opportunity for second language learners to have discourse with native target language peers).
Principle 2: Stages of Second Language Acquisition	▪ There are five stages of language acquisition: pre-production, early production, speech emergence, intermediate fluency, and advanced fluency.	▪ Teachers must recognize the stage of language acquisition that the student is experiencing and be patient with language acquisition. ▪ Teachers should be respectful of the stage the student is experiencing and orchestrate learning around stage progression. ▪ Teachers should understand that even though a student is in the pre-production stage, it is not an indicator of the student's learning or absence of learning.	▪ The capacity building needs to be appropriate for each stage of language acquisition. ▪ For the pre-production stage, teachers need to build student capacity for the receptive domains.	▪ For each stage of language acquisition, the teacher will group students of varying language proficiencies/levels in order to provide a language role model for that specific instructional activity and to build student capacity for language practice and acquisition. ▪ At the pre-production stage, the student will never be forced to speak. Student prompts must respect the pre-production stage and provide alternative means for student expression. ▪ At the early production and speech emergence stages, teachers should use questioning strategies that allow for telegraphic expression while building student vocabulary in order to produce self-expression abilities. ▪ With intermediate and advanced fluency, teachers should employ open-ended questioning strategies to allow students to respond as developmentally and linguistically appropriate.

Table 1.10., continued

Principle	Finding(s)	Classroom Application	Instructional Strategies	Examples of Instructional Strategies

Principle 3: Basic Interpersonal Communication Skills and Cognitive Academic Language Proficiency	• There are two distinct types of language proficiency: Basic Interpersonal Communication Skills (BICS) and Cognitive Academic Language Proficiency (CALP).	• Teachers should not be misled when students are effectively communicating in the social context; this does not mean that a student's academic language proficiency is on the same level as his or her social language proficiency.
		• A student's performance as evidenced by BICS should not be an indicator of his or her CALP.
			• Teachers should provide a broad range of instructional strategies for students to engage in as developmentally and linguistically appropriate.	• Teachers should provide multiple opportunities to build CALP through recursive academic vocabulary acquisition.
				• Strategies should include but not be limited to:
				  ¤ the Frayer Model (Frayer, Frederick, & Klausmeier, 1969),
				  ¤ concept definition mapping (Beck & McKeown, 1991),
				  ¤ Marzano's six-step process for academic vocabulary (Marzano & Pickering, 2005), and
				  ¤ Calderón's seven steps for preteaching vocabulary (Calderón, 2007).

Principle 4: Context-Embedded/Context-Reduced Language and Cognitively Demanding/Undemanding Tasks	• Activities/tasks can be categorized as cognitively demanding/undemanding.
	• A continuum demonstrating the range of the context richness varies from context embedded to context reduced.
		• Teachers should provide as much context as possible when teaching cognitively demanding material.	• Teachers need to make all language context embedded.	• Teachers should use:
				  ▪ visuals,
				  ▪ facial expressions,
				  ▪ gestures,
				  ▪ movement,
				  ▪ manipulatives,
				  ▪ exemplars of successful products, and
				  ▪ interactive activities.

Principle 5: Input Hypothesis	• The input hypothesis establishes comprehensible input (level i + 1), instructs the learner's ability to make meaning out of language, and addresses the emergence of speaking fluency.	• Teachers should teach at level i + 1—using no "dumbed-down" language. • Teachers should understand the importance of a print, discourse, and language-enriched environment. Learning is purposeful, relevant, and interesting.	• Teachers should use simplified language structures accompanied by contextual clues. • Teachers should ensure that the language of the classroom is free of unexplained idiomatic expressions.	• Teachers should incorporate gestures, facial expressions, cognates, realia, graphic organizers, note taking, simplified sentence structures, and visuals while accessing student background knowledge and previous learning in order to provide context for second language acquisition. • Teachers should monitor the language structures taught to ensure that the student is being appropriately challenged in language difficulty in order to achieve comprehensible input.

Table 1.10., continued

Principle	Finding(s)	Classroom Application	Instructional Strategies	Examples of Instructional Strategies
Principle 6: Affective Filter Hypothesis	■ The affective filter hypothesis focuses on the affective conditions in a classroom. Minimal error correction is present, and speaking in the second language is never forced.	■ Students with high motivation and less anxiety are better equipped for second language acquisition. ■ The classroom environment should be one of low stress and high student engagement and motivation. Error correction is achieved through modeling of correct language structures. ■ Differentiated ways for communication exist in the classroom: speaking is never forced.	■ Teachers should ensure that the classroom environment is one of low stress. ■ Teachers need to serve as language role models, always using appropriate, accurate, and correct structures of the majority language.	■ Teachers should organize the classroom in a predictable and fair manner in order to respect the needs of all students. ■ Teachers should provide consistent feedback and encouragement to all students. ■ Teachers should avoid obligating and creating expectations of a student producing a response before the student is capable of or feels comfortable doing so.
Principle 7: Language Transfer Theory	■ L1 has an effect on the acquisition of L2. ■ There are two types of language transfer: positive (facilitation) and negative (inhibition).	■ Teachers need to know the structure of the language systems in order to facilitate positive transfer and address negative transfer. ■ Teachers need to know that negative transfer between two language systems by the student is not always indicative of a language disability.	■ Teachers should become familiar with other language systems that are present in their classroom.	■ Teachers should recognize positive and negative effects of transfer based on their knowledge of the two language systems. ■ Teachers should recognize and predict the trends and patterns of language structure in order to better address issues of transfer. ■ Teachers should teach explicitly those language structures that promote negative transfer in order to access the student's metalinguistic awareness of language.

Table 1.10., continued

Principle	Finding(s)	Classroom Application	Instructional Strategies	Examples of Instructional Strategies
Principle 8: Contexts of Second Language Acquisition	• There are two contexts of second language acquisition: simultaneous and sequential. • The level of L1 is a strong predictor of L2 development.	• Teachers need to understand each student's type of language acquisition. • If errors are presented based on the type of language acquisition, it is not indicative of cognitive failure on the student's part. • If a student is a sequential second language learner, the foundation for a language system is already in place. • If a student is a simultaneous second language learner, the structures are still emerging and will require a different level of differentiation when transfer is involved. • Teachers need to understand the importance of L1 in a student's acquisition of L2.	• Teachers need to differentiate instruction based on the type of language acquisition.	• Teachers need to be proficient at accessing background knowledge and existing language structures for second language acquisition. • For sequential learners, teachers should use cognates, similarities of the language structures, and background knowledge as appropriate. • For simultaneous learners, teachers should teach explicitly both contrasts and comparisons between the two language structures.
Principle 9: Sociocultural Component of Learning	• The Prism Model identifies four components (language development, cognitive development, academic development, and social and cultural processes) necessary for a holistic approach to educating the second language learner.	• Teachers need to know the four components of the Prism Model, which are intricately linked to one another.	• Teachers must ensure that all four components of the Prism Model are in sync for the learner in the classroom.	• Teachers should ensure that language development needs are met for second language learners through the appropriate cognitive and academic instruction. This is coupled with attention to the social and cultural aspects of educating second language learners. • Teachers should view students holistically in order to effectively develop all four components. • Teachers promote a home-to-school connection and maintenance of the first language.

Chapter 2

Giftedness in the CLD Student

The purpose of Chapter 2 is to inform educators of the changing role of assessment when coupled with the country's demographic change to better identify gifted CLD students.

Preview of Standard(s)/Term(s):

- → *NAGC Standard 6: Professional Development: 6.1.1*: Educators systematically participate in ongoing, research-supported professional development that addresses the foundations of gifted education, characteristics of students with gifts and talents, assessment, curriculum planning and instruction, learning environments, and programming.
- → *Blended program practices*: The different instructional methodology or approaches within each type of program, such as bilingual, ESL, and gifted education, that support student learning.
- → *Gifted*: Describes a student who demonstrates both above-average academic ability and high task commitment.
- → *Talented*: Describes a student who demonstrates high task commitment and high creativity or ability in more subjective, nonacademic areas.
- → *Intelligence*: Capacity for learning, reasoning, understanding, and similar forms of mental activity.

➡ *Task commitment*: A student's demonstration of perseverance, dedication, and completion of a task, whether it be academic or centered around a passion.

Introduction

A comprehensive base of knowledge addressing the foundational principles of giftedness is fundamental to best understand how to serve a gifted CLD student. For the classroom teacher who serves CLD students, opportunities to learn about the principles of giftedness may have never been presented. Most states required some form of rudimentary professional development, which may or may not be completed prior to a teacher's assignment of working with a gifted student. Some schools practice the insipid rule of thumb that a linguistically diverse student cannot be gifted until he has acquired English language proficiency and, therefore, no professional development in gifted education is needed by the teacher until that point (if at all). This is unequivocally false; giftedness defies linguistic boundaries. The key to addressing giftedness in the CLD student is in the ability to recognize and develop potential. The foundational piece of teaching students who have been identified and served under two types of programs is the understanding that the development of gifted potential is achieved through a blending, or the integration, of programs. In education, program disciplines are identified by the types of services provided to students and through specific program models (e.g., bilingual education, English as a second language, gifted and talented education), and students are categorized by the types of services they receive, such as English language learners (ELLs) or gifted. Many students receive a plethora of services throughout their tenure in school, all for the purpose of increasing their achievement.

Program instructional practices are validated through foundational principles, which are developed through research, practice, and service and provide a basis for understanding and categorizing the services provided by the discipline. The continuing change in student demographics demands that all educators serving CLD students be proficient in both gifted education as well as second language acquisition, thereby blending program practices in both fields and holistically integrating services to meet whatever educational need or combination thereof that a gifted CLD student may have and deserve.

Program disciplines present in the culturally and linguistically diverse classroom include:
- ✔ second language acquisition and
- ✔ giftedness.

Although the program practices of second language acquisition, identification of gifted potential, and serving the gifted are the most pertinent to the CLD classroom, they are not mutually exclusive.

Changing Role of Assessment

It is not a matter of whether giftedness exists among bilingual, poor children, but a matter of sensitivity of evaluators and the instruments they select to use for a specific purpose and in a specific manner.

—Virginia González

The purpose of this section is not to call into question the validity of standardized assessments used for identification and their impact on CLD students. However, CLD students do feel the impact of assessment when the administration of the test and the results, which are used to make decisions about student giftedness, are biased. As student demographics change, sensitivity surrounding the assessment of CLD students must evolve in order to accurately identify potential giftedness in CLD students.

Renzulli (1979) captured the essence of defining giftedness and the issue of change in the matter of assessment:

> As the definition of giftedness is extended beyond those abilities that are clearly reflected in tests of intelligence, achievement, and academic aptitude, it becomes necessary to put *less emphasis* on precise estimates of performance and potential and *more emphasis* on the opinions of qualified persons in making decisions about admission to special programs. The crux of the issue boils down to a simple and yet very important question: How much of a trade-off are we willing to make on the objective to subjective continuum in order to allow recognition of a broader spectrum of human abilities? (p. 181, emphasis added)

The reality of gifted education is that standardized assessment is most often used to determine program qualification. The greater issue is the underlying assumption that assessment is equitable and that the teacher is able to recognize and identify giftedness. If a teacher is not well versed in both second language acquisition and gifted education, then the opportunity for CLD students to be identified and reach their gifted potential is diminished.

The teacher's role is multifaceted, ranging (in many instances) from that of the initial assessor to instructor to student advocate. The fact that the demographics of the student population are changing rapidly and teachers often lack specialized training complicates this matter.

Teacher competency requires:
✔ understanding of assessment with CLD students and
✔ working knowledge of gifted education.

For there to be equity in the identification process for CLD students, there are five merit statements that must be embraced and incorporated into all aspects of the process.

➡ A student may be gifted and bilingual.
➡ Giftedness is found in all language groups.
➡ Students are not less intellectual or less gifted if they do not speak the majority language.
➡ Gifted services should not be contingent on majority language proficiency.
➡ Assessment should be about identifying giftedness and not majority language ability.

These merit statements set the tone for the operational context of the school and identification of gifted CLD students. Standardized tests used for identification of CLD students for gifted education are the most common instrument available to gifted and talented programs. However, for the CLD student, a standardized test does not always provide the appropriate venue for measuring that student's giftedness.

In order to build teacher competence, eight foundational principles of gifted and talented education have been identified. A working knowledge of these principles provides educators with an understanding of the foundation needed for working with potentially gifted students.

Principle 1: The Marland Report

Education of the Gifted and Talented, the federal report referred to as the Marland Report, named after then U.S. Commissioner of Education Sidney Marland, was submitted to Congress in 1972 as a call to awareness for equity in gifted education services. The Marland Report's importance is threefold. First, it called for greater services to diverse groups of students who had been historically underrepresented in gifted education. Second, it provided a federal definition of gifted and talented. The report defined gifted and talented children as:

> those identified by professionally qualified persons who, by virtue of outstanding abilities, are capable of high performance. These are children who require differential educational programs and/or services beyond those provided by the regular school program in order to realize their contribution to self and the society.
>
> Children capable of high performance include those with demonstrated achievement and/or potential ability in any of the following areas, singly or in combination:
> 1. General intellectual ability
> 2. Specific academic aptitude
> 3. Creative or productive thinking
> 4. Leadership ability
> 5. Visual and performing arts
> 6. Psychomotor ability. (Marland, 1972, pp. 10–11)

Third, it coupled federal regulations for service with funding. At that time, school districts quickly adopted the definition of gifted and talented and the parameters for service and funding. Incorporating the tenets of the Marland Report at the local school district level serves as the foundation of gifted and talented education. Table 2.1 highlights this principle.

Principle 2: Three-Ring Conception of Giftedness

Although many local school districts continue to use the Marland Report as a basis for defining giftedness, experts in the field have also impacted the evolving process of identifying gifted students. In 1986, Dr. Joseph Renzulli published a model that shifted away from the narrower, exclusive definitions of giftedness that had been used in past research and only focused on academic achievement and aptitude. Renzulli's Three-Ring Conception of Giftedness illustrates that creativity and task commitment, or perseverance with the topic

Table 2.1
Principle 1: The Marland Report

Researcher(s)	Finding(s)	Classroom Application(s)
Marland (1972)	• The Marland Report was a call for greater services to diverse groups of students who had been historically underrepresented in gifted education. • It established a definition of gifted and talented children. • The report helped couple federal regulations for service with funding.	• Teachers are labeled as professionally qualified persons who identify children that are gifted and talented. • Gifted children, once identified, require differentiated educational programs and/or services beyond those normally provided by the regular school program in order to realize their contribution to self and society.

at hand, should be considered in addition to above-average ability (often measured with IQ and cognitive ability tests) in the identification of potentially gifted individuals. Renzulli (1986) underscored the interaction of the three rings in the development of giftedness. "This point is emphasized because one of the major errors that continues to be made in identification procedures is to overemphasize superior abilities at the expense of the other two clusters of traits" (Renzulli, 1986, p. 259). Therefore, giftedness, illustrated in the model by the small surface at the overlap of all three rings, is a result of the interaction of above-average ability, creativity, and task commitment (see Figure 2.1). Table 2.2 highlights this principle.

Principle 3: Social and Emotional Development for the Gifted

In the early 20th century, the idea of tailoring instruction to fit the intellectual needs of gifted students began to evolve and establish itself as a specialized discipline in the field of education. Through the work of psychologist Leta Hollingworth (1926), a pioneer in gifted education research, educators discovered that in addition to specific academic needs, gifted students also have social and emotional needs that cannot be ignored. According to Hollingworth, highly gifted students (above 180 IQ in her research) in particular may suffer from isolation due to the inability to identify with and socialize with their peers. Hollingworth (1936) noted:

> This difficulty of the gifted child in forming friendships is largely a result of the infrequency of persons who are like-minded. The more intelligent a person is, regardless of age,

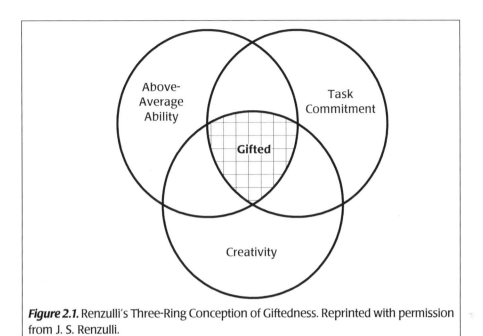

Figure 2.1. Renzulli's Three-Ring Conception of Giftedness. Reprinted with permission from J. S. Renzulli.

Table 2.2
Principle 2: Three-Ring Conception of Giftedness

Researcher(s)	Finding(s)	Classroom Application(s)
Renzulli (1986)	• Although students who have the potential for giftedness display above-average ability, creativity and task commitment must not be overlooked. Giftedness involves the interface of each of these three areas.	• Teachers should understand that creativity of thought evidenced during classroom experiences as well as levels of task commitment displayed by a student can be indicators of gifted potential. • Educators should use caution when identifying giftedness using only above-average ability as the sole indicator.

the less often can he find a truly congenial companion. The average child finds playmates in plenty who can think and act on a level congenial to him, because there are so many average children. (p. 279)

The social and emotional development and adjustment of gifted children are an essential component of addressing and meeting their overall needs. Table 2.3 highlights this principle.

Table 2.3
Principle 3: Social and Emotional Development for the Gifted

Researcher(s)	Finding(s)	Classroom Application(s)
Hollingworth (1926, 1936)	• Gifted children have specific social and emotional needs that need to be addressed. • Highly gifted children often have difficulties developing peer relationships because of the struggle in identifying others who are like-minded.	• Educators who make decisions and/or give input about a gifted child's schooling need to have knowledge of the social and emotional issues that are often associated with being gifted. • Gifted children seek intellectual peers that can understand their complex ideas. Often, such intellectual peers are much older children or adults. Gifted children would like nothing more than to "fit in" with a peer group their own age; however, many times same-age peers cannot relate to the thoughts and/or behaviors of gifted children.

Principle 4: Creative and Critical Thinking

Creative and critical thinking are interwoven throughout all of the elements of gifted education. Best instructional practices aim to ensure that the gifted student has every opportunity to apply his level of creativity to the school task at hand and that critical thinking is incorporated throughout each and every instructional activity. In their book, *Creative Problem Solving: The Basic Course*, Isaksen and Treffinger (1985) described the differences between creative and critical thinking and provided a six-step process for problem solving (see Table 2.4). These steps are important when planning classroom activities in order to achieve optimal creative and critical thinking. Table 2.4 highlights this principle.

Principle 5: Autonomous Learner Model

The Autonomous Learner Model (ALM) by George Betts (1985) is designed to meet the diverse cognitive, emotional, and social needs of the gifted and talented learner through five major dimensions: orientation, individual development, enrichment, seminars, and in-depth studies (see Figure 2.2). The dimensions describe the quality, duration, and type of learning in which gifted students should be participating at school. Table 2.5 highlights this principle.

Principle 6: The Integrated Curriculum Model

Joyce VanTassel-Baska developed the Integrated Curriculum Model (ICM) as a framework for gifted education (see Figure 2.3). The ICM illustrates the need for balance among the advanced content, the overarching concepts/

Table 2.4
Principle 4: Creative and Critical Thinking

Researcher(s)	Finding(s)	Classroom Application(s)
Isaksen and Treffinger (1985)	• Creative thinking is defined as making and communicating connections to think of many new and unusual possibilities, which provide guidance in generating and selecting alternatives. • Critical thinking is described as analyzing and developing possibilities to: (a) compare and contrast ideas, (b) improve and refine ideas, (c) make effective decisions and judgments, and (d) provide a sound foundation for effective action.	• There is a six-step process for problem solving: 1. Mess Finding 2. Data Finding 3. Problem Finding 4. Idea Finding 5. Solution Finding 6. Acceptance Finding

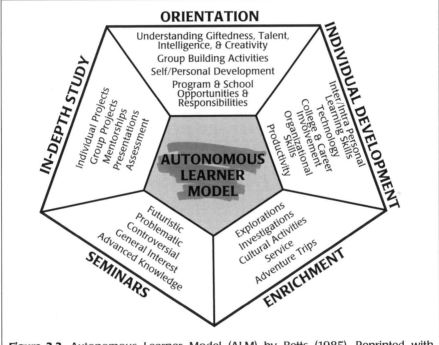

Figure 2.2. Autonomous Learner Model (ALM) by Betts (1985). Reprinted with permission from G. Betts.

themes, and the learning process-product dimensions of gifted education. The interrelated dimensions of the ICM clearly show that no one dimension has more value than the other. Themes/big ideas have no more value than the content topics, the processes that are used, or the products developed to make sense of them. VanTassel-Baska (1986, 1995) noted it is this "comfortable blending" of the three dimensions that makes gifted curriculum effective. Table 2.6 highlights this principle.

Table 2.5
Principle 5: Autonomous Learner Model

Researcher(s)	Finding(s)	Classroom Application(s)
Betts (1985)	▪ The cognitive, emotional, and social needs of the gifted and talented learner can be met through the dimensions provided in the Autonomous Learner Model (ALM).	▪ *Dimension 1: Orientation*—Foundational understanding of giftedness is provided to all stakeholders. Self-awareness and awareness of others is developed. ▪ *Dimension 2: Individual Development*—Lifelong learning skills coupled with the area of technology are developed in the gifted student. Students become autonomous in their learning. ▪ *Dimension 3: Enrichment*—Students explore content outside of the school curriculum that is self-selected. Service learning is a component of this dimension. ▪ *Dimension 4: Seminars*—Opportunities for learners to research a topic and then teach it to others is vital in transforming each learner. Seminars are student led and topics are student selected. ▪ *Dimension 5: In-Depth Studies*—Students are given the opportunity to select long-term, in-depth content area studies. Students present their learning at the end of the study.

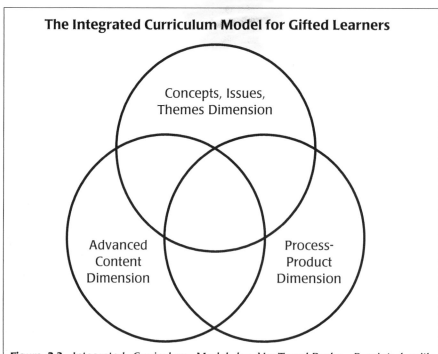

Figure 2.3. Integrated Curriculum Model by VanTassel-Baska. Reprinted with permission from the Center for Gifted Education.

Table 2.6
Principle 6: The Integrated Curriculum Model

Researcher(s)	Finding(s)	Classroom Application(s)
VanTassel-Baska (1986, 1995)	▪ Dimensions of concepts, issues, themes, advanced content, and process-product are interrelated as educators respond to the gifted and talented characteristics of precocity, intensity, and complexity.	▪ Instructional differentiation can come in any form of advanced content and/or be interdisciplinary. Such differentiation often takes the form of broad overarching issues, themes, and/or concepts; the process by which content is learned; the product produced that demonstrates understanding; and/or variations in the learning environment.

Principle 7: Differentiated Instruction

As opposed to a one-size-fits-all mindset to classroom teaching, gifted educators advocate for differentiated instruction. *Differentiation* means that classroom instruction is purposefully designed to match each student's readiness level, interest level, and learning style. In this approach, the teacher utilizes a variety of methods to help each student master curriculum standards, thoughtfully choosing what content will be learned, how that content will be explored, and how understanding will be demonstrated. Essentially, learning for each student can be differentiated through content, process, and product (Tomlinson, 1995).

Curriculum standards (what students are to learn) guide the key concepts, information, and/or skills of a particular unit of study. Within these standards, emphasis is placed on students making sense of their own learning and understanding the key principles associated within the required unit. Often, curriculum standards are skill based. Therefore, depending on the format of the unit/course, content may be arranged around a theme or essential question(s), chronologically, or in an interdisciplinary format. In each scenario, the curriculum standards can naturally be woven into the chosen instructional framework.

Process is the way by which students come to understand or "own" new information via engaging, instructional activities. The teacher purposefully plans these activities after considering the readiness level, skill level, interest level, and learning styles of the students in the classroom. Tiered lessons are often designed to utilize instructional strategies that allow for individual, paired, small-group, and some whole-group investigation and/or instruction. It is in this area that choice becomes imperative to ensure student engagement and interaction with the curriculum content (Tomlinson, 1995).

The product component of differentiation provides an opportunity, via assessment or demonstration, for a student to show what she has come to know, understand, or be able to do as a result of recent classroom learning. Understanding and mastery of the content associated with the curriculum standards can be demonstrated in numerous ways. Assessment is not limited to the traditional end-of-unit test but can instead be a culminating project, a combination of smaller activities, and/or a collection of work that shows competency, growth, and transfer of knowledge throughout the unit of study or an even larger span of time. Through the product component of differentiation, teachers can give students the opportunity to produce authentic work as a result of meaningful, respectful teacher-facilitated instruction.

In summary, differentiated instruction is not a one-size-fits-all model of instruction and does not mean more work for those gifted learners who finish assignments more quickly than their classmates. Differentiated instruction is different, respectful, engaging, and responsive instructional activities for each learner. Differentiated instruction requires a skilled educator who is willing to do the bulk of the classroom planning and preparation ahead of time and slip into a facilitator/learning partner role when the students enter the classroom. Table 2.7 highlights this principle.

Principle 8: Depth and Complexity

Obtaining knowledge on a certain topic in order to recall it for an end-of-unit test no longer provides the type of learning the 21st century demands. Learners today need to be able to make meaningful connections between what they learn in the classroom and what they encounter daily via interactions with peers, adults, text, and media in our shrinking global society. In an attempt to move gifted learners to deeper levels of contextual understanding and authentic transfer of knowledge, Kaplan (1997) developed the elements of depth and complexity. It is with these elements that Kaplan sought to assist teachers in guiding students toward academic excellence and scholarliness (Lafferty, n.d.).

According to Kaplan (1997), *depth* refers to the elaboration within a discipline and *complexity* refers to building understanding across disciplines, over time, and from multiple perspectives. Depth can be best understood by exploring the following elements of a given discipline: the language, details, rules, patterns, trends, unanswered questions, ethics, and big ideas (i.e., generalizations, principles, theories). Complexity then develops from looking at subjects over time, across disciplines, and from different points of view. With each of the previously mentioned elements, guiding key questions assist learners in understanding and making logical connections to the content, thereby producing students who are able to analyze and synthesize the world around them. Table 2.8 highlights this principle.

Table 2.7
Principle 7: Differentiated Instruction

Researcher	Finding(s)	Classroom Application(s)
Tomlinson (1995, 1999)	▪ Students need relevant content combined with engaging instruction and challenging assignments.	▪ Different does not mean more. ▪ Classroom work needs to be respectful and purposeful. ▪ Teachers must understand and know all of the students equally. ▪ Assessment and instruction often must happen simultaneously. ▪ Differentiate content, process, and product in relationship to the students' readiness and interests. ▪ Teachers select a concept from the curriculum and design differentiated lessons for the student.

Table 2.8
Principle 8: Depth and Complexity

Researcher(s)	Finding(s)	Classroom Application(s)

Kaplan (1997)	▪ There are various tools used to build curricular depth and complexity:
	  ¤ details;
	  ¤ patterns;
	  ¤ trends;
	  ¤ rules;
	  ¤ ethics;
	  ¤ unanswered questions;
	  ¤ big ideas;
	  ¤ relationships across time, and across and within disciplines; and
	  ¤ point of view.
		▪ Depth refers to the exploration within a discipline.
		▪ Complexity refers to building understanding across disciplines, over time, and from multiple perspectives.
		▪ When seeking greater understanding of the world in which one lives, the depth and complexity model can assist with raising academic rigor both within and between disciplines.

A New Model

The development of gifted and talented programs has prompted an evolution in the definitions for a gifted student. A review of these definitions suggests a wide spectrum of criteria by which the eligibility of a potential candidate is determined. More conservative views uphold achievement scores that measure academic abilities as the defining factor of a gifted student. This strictly quantitative notion would support the traditional label of "gifted." Other researchers and practitioners consider additional abilities, such as creativity, leadership, and fine arts, to be equally viable avenues for qualifying for gifted programs. This view can generally be associated with the "talented" student. The question that then begs to be asked is how can the two aforementioned views be combined fairly to identify a student's gifted potential, no matter the language spoken or culture in which one was raised?

In an attempt to marry the two terms of *gifted* and *talented* to produce a more accurate depiction of giftedness, Renzulli (1986) developed the Three-Ring Conception of Giftedness. As outlined previously in Principle 2, Renzulli's model visually highlights the area where gifted potential exists as represented by the intersection of above-average (or high) ability, high amounts of creativity, and high levels of task commitment. What Renzulli's model does not account for is what giftedness "looks like" in the gifted underachiever nor how the academic overachiever can mistakenly be identified as gifted. Terms such as *underachiever* and *overachiever* add to the haziness in the continued quest to define giftedness and then accurately identify gifted potential in children. As authors of this book, we believe the way to do this is to define gifted potential to include both a definition of gifted and a definition of talented. Like Renzulli, we believe the three essential components to defining gifted and talented are found in the areas of ability, creativity, and task commitment. However, in an effort to clarify the defining features of a gifted and talented student, one must consider the notion of the overachieving and underachieving student. To account for the four, separate components of our gifted and talented definition, we have developed a model to demonstrate the interface of these terms.

We begin by recognizing that although Renzulli's (1986) Three-Ring Conception of Giftedness validates the need for and recognizes the idea of task commitment, his model does not offer a way to visually represent this idea as it applies to the over- or underachieving child. Hence, using Renzulli's theory as a base model, there is a need for something that visually represents the idea that task commitment should be factored into both gifted and talented definitions when used as an identification tool to represent gifted potential.

Our interpretation of Renzulli's (1986) Three Ring Conception of Giftedness model, called the Gifted and Talented Interface Model (see Figure 2.4), shows that a gifted student demonstrates both above-average academic ability and high task commitment. A talented student demonstrates high task commitment and high creativity or ability in more subjective, nonacademic areas. Thus, a truly "gifted and talented" individual exhibits high academic ability, creativity, and task commitment. However, for centuries, educators have witnessed the common phenomenon of the extremely bright student with very little task commitment (motivation) and/or the extremely talented student who lacks the necessary task commitment (motivation) to perform to his or her full potential.

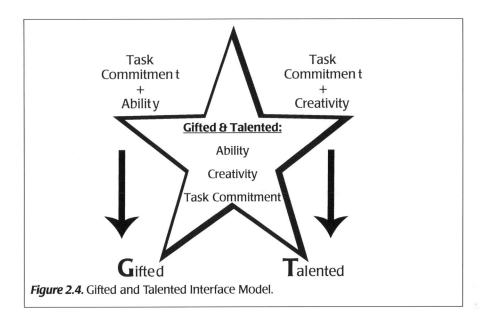

Figure 2.4. Gifted and Talented Interface Model.

The defining elements in the identification of a gifted and/or talented student are academic ability and creativity, respectively. However, an individual's level of task commitment further classifies the student. If gifted or talented students show low task commitment, their true abilities are concealed, resulting in underachievement. On the other extreme, students who demonstrate high task commitment coupled with average academic ability or creativity often characterize what some might consider to be overachievement. The arrows in Figure 2.5 represent the various levels of academic ability, task commitment, and creativity. The clarified relationships among these terms can help resolve the extensive debate surrounding how to define a gifted and talented student.

The contemporary gifted educator embraces opportunities to identify giftedness in culturally diverse students through nontraditional approaches. Applying historical principles of gifted education and second language acquisition leads to new educator perspectives, broader definitions of giftedness, and modified assessment methods.

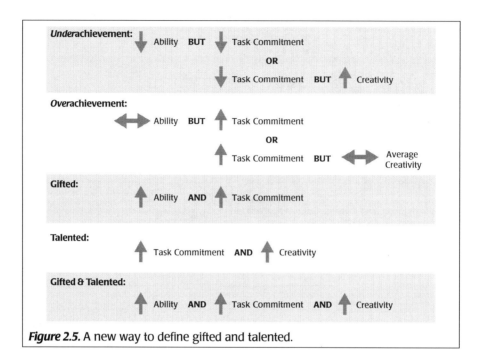

Figure 2.5. A new way to define gifted and talented.

Section II:

Examining Existing Programmatic Structures

Chapter 3

CLD Representation in Gifted Programs

The purpose of Chapter 3 is to help educators develop a different perspective on identifying potential giftedness in CLD students and to ensure that there is no population over- or underrepresented in gifted and talented programs based on campus demographics.

Preview of Standard(s)/Term(s):

➻ *NAGC Standard 2: Assessment*: Assessments provide information about identification, learning progress and outcomes, and evaluation of programming for students with gifts and talents in all domains.

➻ *Language neutral*: The context of the activity or student learning to be demonstrated does not rely on language for understanding.

➻ *Overrepresentation*: This occurs when a student population is larger in representation in the service group in comparison to its representation in the general population.

➻ *Underrepresentation*: This occurs when a student population is smaller in representation in the service group in comparison to its representation in the general population.

➻ *Task commitment*: A student's demonstration of perseverance, dedication, and completion of task, whether it be academic or centered around a passion or necessity.

➻ *Innate ability*: One's own natural aptitude.

- ➤ *Learner ability*: A student's potential cognitive development influenced by environment and/or schooling.
- ➤ *Interest saturation*: The intense exploration of one's passion.
- ➤ *Authentic work experiences*: Orchestrated opportunities for students to demonstrate their understanding, knowledge, and/or ability to synthesize learning.
- ➤ *School performance*: The outcome of student effort on a given task.
- ➤ *Multipronged identification process*: A menu of assessment instruments that value authentic thought, culture, and creativity, using language neutral methods.

Changing Demographics

The public school system's ability to respond to the challenge of educating the fastest growing population of students, the culturally and linguistically diverse, is imperative to the long-term sustainability of the system. According to the U.S. Census Bureau, in 2007, approximately 69% of Hispanic and 64% of Asian elementary and secondary school students spoke a language other than English at home. Approximately 18% of Hispanic and 17% of Asian students spoke English with difficulty, compared with 7% of Native Hawaiians or Other Pacific Islanders, 3% of American Indians/Alaska Natives, and 1% each of Whites and Blacks, according to household reports (U.S. Census Bureau, 2007). As the national demographics continue to become more culturally and linguistically diverse, public education must advance programs that serve students learning English as a second language.

As school organizations reel from the impact of these changing demographics, little attention is given to moving past the first fundamental steps of educating CLD students. The educational emphasis becomes administrative, and state-mandated testing drives the course of learning. When competing for dwindling resources, exemplar programs that effectively meet the cultural and linguistic needs of CLD students are scarce. Language immersion programs that maintain the integrity of additive bilingualism and the cultural dignity of students from diverse backgrounds are under constant scrutiny; all the while, their demonstrated educational benefit is considered a best practice for educating linguistically diverse students.

The driving force of English acquisition subsumes the critical need to differentiate and develop services beyond language for the gifted CLD student. It leads to critical errors in the identification of CLD students.

Reviewing Campus-Level Data

The first step in correcting critical errors in the identification of gifted CLD students requires reflecting on existing practices and informed decision making regarding CLD representation. Intentional review of current practices in identifying gifted CLD students begins with ensuring that the identification measures and instruments are language neutral. CLD students should have the opportunity to demonstrate their abilities in a context that does not rely on the second language as a measurement. The student's gifted potential is revealed through activities that are not language based, rather than potential being postponed until English proficiency is reached. Waiting until a linguistically diverse student acquires English to determine her potential giftedness is an inherently biased and educationally unsound practice. To base gifted program services on English proficiency is to deny access to educational services.

To address program equity and access for CLD students, the percentage of these students participating in gifted services at each grade level should be reviewed annually. The percentage of CLD students participating in gifted services should reflect the demographic representation of the CLD student population at the campus level—not over or under. Based on the review results, the appropriateness of the identification and service process can be determined. A large overrepresentation is as great of a misstep as underrepresentation and indicates failure in the identification system as well.

A review of the enrollment and program service data can be easily accomplished to determine if there is equitable student demographic representation in the gifted and talented program. To begin the review, the following data are gathered:

- total campus enrollment,
- the number of students enrolled at the campus representing each ethnicity,
- ethnic representation (percentage) of the total campus enrollment,
- total number of students served in the gifted and talented program services, and
- ethnic representation of students in the gifted and talented program (how many students are participating from each ethnic group in the gifted and talented program).

Table 3.1 demonstrates how the data may be organized for the review.

Once the percentage of CLD students being served in a gifted education program is identified, determining whether or not an ethnicity is equitably represented is straightforward. A campus's overall ethnicity percentages should be closely reflected in the ethnic percentages served in the program. This is represented by the columns shown in Table 3.1: actual number versus number needed. To determine the number needed to reach representation, multiply the percentage needed to reach representation by the gifted and talented student enrollment. For example, in the African American student scenario, the percent needed to reach equitable representation in gifted education is 15%. The number of students in gifted education is 54. Apply the process as outlined above: 15% x 54 = 8.1. Therefore, a minimum of 8 African American students would need to be represented in the campus's gifted education program in order for that ethnicity to be considered equitably represented in light of the campus population. Once a campus identifies the number of students actually being served from each student demographic, educators can compare each of these numbers to the total percentage of students in the overall campus demographics.

Table 3.2 looks at the additional issue of over- versus underrepresentation. Areas where student demographics are over- and underrepresented are provided. Both areas (over and under) demand consideration by campus and program administration. Although it is not always reasonable to compute exact percentages of campus to student program ethnicity, the review of data ensures that potential giftedness in culturally and linguistically diverse student groups is not overlooked, and these students are not precluded from service.

When comparing each population's total enrollment to the actual percentage of students enrolled in a gifted program, it is easy to identify enrollment discrepancies. Overrepresentation exists when the percentage of those identified exceeds the percentage of the total campus population. Conversely, underrepresentation occurs when the percentage of those identified falls below the percentage represented in the total campus population. In the case of underrepresentation of CLD students, the Gifted and Talented Interface Model can be used as a philosophical foundation for rethinking equity in the gifted and talented identification process.

Shifting the Identification Thought Process

One way to begin shifting the identification process would be to consider the definition of gifted and talented as presented in the Gifted and Talented Interface Model. The shift is represented metaphorically by the "GT Watch,"

Table 3.1
Organizing Data for Review

	African American		Hispanic		White		Pacific Islander		American Indian		Asian	
	Campus Student Population: 93 (15%)		Campus Student Population: 180 (29%)		Campus Student Population: 227 (37%)		Campus Student Population: 15 (2%)		Campus Student Population: 6 (1%)		Campus Student Population: 92 (15%)	
	Actual Number in GT Program	Number Needed to Reach Representation	Actual Number in GT Program	Number Needed to Reach Representation	Actual Number in GT Program	Number Needed to Reach Representation	Actual Number in GT Program	Number Needed to Reach Representation	Actual Number in GT Program	Number Needed to Reach Representation	Actual Number in GT Program	Number Needed to Reach Representation
Campus Total Enrollment: 613												
GT Program Enrollment: 54 (8%)	5 (10%)	8 (15%)	7 (13%)	16 (29%)	35 (65%)	20 (37%)	0 (0%)	1 (2%)	0 (0%)	1 (1%)	7 (13%)	8 (15%)

Table 3.2
Over- Versus Underrepresentation

	African American		Hispanic		White		Pacific Islander		American Indian		Asian	
	Campus Student Population: 93 (15%)		Campus Student Population: 180 (29%)		Campus Student Population: 227 (37%)		Campus Student Population: 15 (2%)		Campus Student Population: 6 (1%)		Campus Student Population: 92 (15%)	
	Actual Number in GT Program	Number Needed to Reach Representation	Actual Number in GT Program	Number Needed to Reach Representation	Actual Number in GT Program	Number Needed to Reach Representation	Actual Number in GT Program	Number Needed to Reach Representation	Actual Number in GT Program	Number Needed to Reach Representation	Actual Number in GT Program	Number Needed to Reach Representation
Campus Total Enrollment: 613												
GT Program Enrollment: 54 (8%)	5 (10%)	8 (15%)	7 (13%)	16 (29%)	35 (65%)	20 (37%)	0 (0%)	1 (2%)	0 (0%)	1 (1%)	7 (13%)	8 (15%)
Over (+) Under (−)	−		−		+		−		−		−	

which considers ability/creative and task commitment to indicate the giftedness of the individual in a language neutral manner. A new way of considering a potential student for gifted services in terms of his or her ability/creativity and task commitment, the GT Watch visual can be used to distinguish between innate ability and levels of task commitment. This visual metaphor greater defines who is truly gifted or talented for more accurate identification purposes. The left side of the watch face corresponds to the levels of innate or learned ability exhibited by the student, regardless of language, and the right side denotes his or her level of task commitment. The horizontal axis from 9 to 3 signifies the norm (average) of the student's peers for ability/creativity and task commitment, respectively (see Figure 3.1).

If the level of ability (or creativity) is denoted by the hour hand, a student who scores below the norm for ability would rest somewhere between the 6 o'clock and 9 o'clock hours. Conversely, if the student scores above average as compared to his or her peer group, the hour hand would fall between the 9 o'clock and 12 o'clock hours (see Figure 3.2). The 12 o'clock mark represents the highest achievement score possible; the closer the hour hand reads toward 12 o'clock, the more "gifted" or "talented" the student is.

A student's level of task commitment is symbolized by the minute hand. The minute hand of a student who exhibits a high level of task commitment would fall between 12 o'clock and 3 o'clock (see Figure 3.3). The minute hand of a student who exhibits a level of task commitment below the norm, as compared to his or her peers, would fall between 3 o'clock and 6 o'clock.

A gifted student is one who has a high level of ability, whether learned or innate, coupled with a high level of task commitment. The hour hand is geared in between 9 o'clock and 12 o'clock, and the minute hand is placed somewhere between 12 o'clock and 3 o'clock. The gifted or talented student is represented by 10:10. Overachieving students are characterized by extremely high level of task commitment, although their abilities may only be average or slightly above average. The overachiever is illustrated by 9 o'clock. On the other hand, an underachiever is depicted by 10:30, as he or she has above-average ability, but does not display task commitment. See Figure 3.4 for a visual representation of these students.

A student who is both gifted and talented is represented by the 12 o'clock time. He or she displays high levels of both creativity and ability. Although his or her task commitment may vary, for illustrative purposes, the student shall be categorized as 12 o'clock (see Figure 3.5).

To initiate a philosophical shift to this broader definition of gifted and talented, this new definition can be represented by the GT Watch using current district assessment tools. No matter what the assessment tools, the process

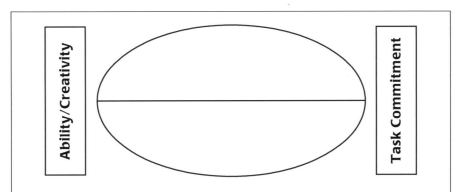

Figure 3.1. The GT Watch's 9–3 horizontal axis: Baseline for average ability or creativity.

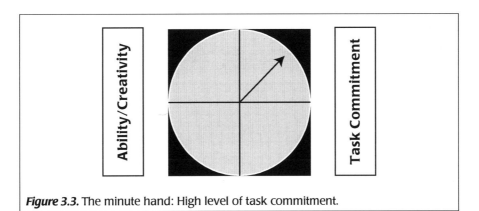

Below-Average Ability/Creativity

Above-Average Ability/Creativity

Figure 3.2. Below- and above-average visual representations.

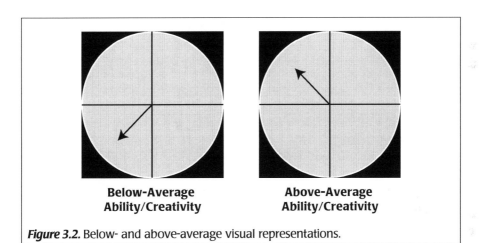

Figure 3.3. The minute hand: High level of task commitment.

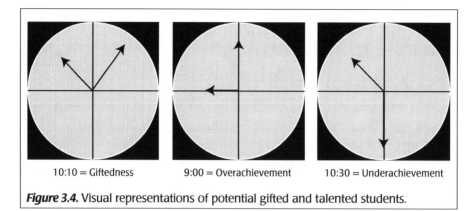

| 10:10 = Giftedness | 9:00 = Overachievement | 10:30 = Underachievement |

Figure 3.4. Visual representations of potential gifted and talented students.

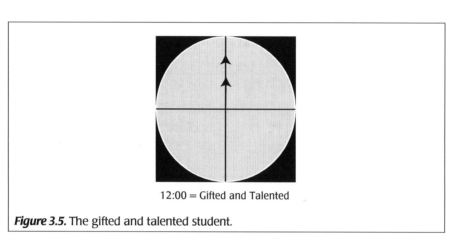

12:00 = Gifted and Talented

Figure 3.5. The gifted and talented student.

of making that philosophical shift comes when considering the relationships between a child's ability, creativity, and task commitment. The watch and its hands serve as visual rubrics for the identification process. Districts and campuses may use the GT Watch to visually clarify how the levels of student task commitment contribute to the overall perception of levels of ability and creativity for identification purposes.

Shifting Assessment Practices

The following principles are involved in shifting the thought paradigm for CLD identification processes and were incorporated as guidelines in designing an identification rubric to ensure equity in the identification process (Richert, 1985):

⟿ *Defensibility*: Procedures should be based on the best available research and recommendations.

→ *Advocacy*: Identification should be designed in the best interest of all students.

→ *Equity*: Procedures should guarantee that no one is overlooked and strategies for identifying the underrepresented should be specific.

→ *Pluralism*: The broadest defensible definition of gifted and talented should be used.

→ *Comprehensiveness*: As many learners as possible with gifted and talented potential should be identified and served.

→ *Pragmatism*: Whenever possible, procedures should allow for the cost-effective modification and use of available instruments and personnel.

Although, metaphorically, the hands of the watch would be positioned for the CLD student in the same manner, equity in the identification process for CLD students can be addressed by examining the assessment instruments used in that process. What "counts" when representing ability, creativity, and task commitment? Table 3.3 is an attempt to connect the familiar assessment tools with this revised conception of the identification process for gifted and talented services.

As represented in Table 3.3, many assessment instruments exist to identify the gifted and talented and/or those with gifted potential. To ensure selection of appropriate assessment instruments, the following considerations were recommended (Richert, 1985):

→ Select different measures and procedures to identify each diverse gifted ability.

→ Address these issues before using any test:

  ↪ Is the test appropriate for the ability being sought?

  ↪ Is the test being used at the appropriate stage of identification (e.g., nomination into a broad talent pool, assessment for a specific program option, evaluation within a program)?

→ Is the test appropriate for underrepresented subpopulations within the district (e.g., students from economically disadvantaged backgrounds, minority students, underachievers)?

The Gifted and Talented Interface Model does not support using a single ability indicator as a sole qualifier for gifted services. Instead, the model represents a multipronged, inclusive process that embraces a broader definition of gifted and talented students. The Gifted and Talented Interface Model could be implemented at a district level to establish protocols for the identification process. The district would then expect campuses to be consistent in the types

Table 3.3
Assessment Table

| Ability | | Creativity Task Commitment |
Innate Ability (Quantitative)	Learned Ability (Quantitative)	(Qualitative)
Cognitive Abilities Test Form 6 (CogAT)	Comprehensive Scales of Student Ability (CSSA)	Gifted Evaluation Scale
Cognitive Abilities Test Nonverbal Battery (CoGAT Nonverbal)	Iowa Tests of Basic Skills, Form M (ITBS)	Group Inventory for Finding Interests
Bilingual Verbal Ability Tests (BVAT)	Kaufman Test of Educational Achievement (K-TEA-NU)	Group Inventory for Finding Talent (GIFT)
Comprehensive Test of Nonverbal Intelligence (CTONI)	Metropolitan Achievement Tests, 8th Edition (Metro-8)	Iowa Acceleration Scale (IAS)
Das-Naglieri Cognitive Assessment System (CAS)	Mini-Battery of Achievement	Kingore Observation Inventory (KOI)
Differential Ability Scales (DAS)	Stanford Achievement Test, 9th Edition (SAT-9); Aprenda-2 (SAT Spanish)	Authentic work experiences
Gifted and Talented Evaluation Scale (GATES)	State proficiency tests	Interest saturation
Leiter International Performance Scale–Revised (Leiter-R)	Wechsler Individual Achievement Test, 2nd Edition (WIAT-II)	Parent recommendation, anecdotes, and/or letter of advocacy
Naglieri Nonverbal Ability Test Multilevel Form (NNAT)	Woodcock-Johnson III Tests of Achievement (WJ-III)	Teacher recommendation, anecdotes, and/or letter of advocacy
Otis-Lennon School Abilities Test, 7th edition (OLSAT-7)	Language screening results	Various characteristics checklists
Screening Assessment for Gifted Elementary and Middle School Students, 2nd edition (SAGES-2)	Awards, recognitions, and achievements	
Stanford-Binet Intelligence, Form L-M		Writing samples
Structure of Intellect Test of Learning Abilities (SOI)		
Test of Nonverbal Intelligence, 4th Edition (TONI-4)		
Torrance Tests of Creative Thinking (TTCT) Figural and Verbal	School performance	
Universal Nonverbal Intelligence Test (UNIT)		Portfolio of student work
Wechsler Intelligence Scale for Children, 3rd Edition (WISC-III)		
Woodcock-Johnson III Tests of Cognitive Abilities (WJ-III)		

Note. Adapted from Slocumb (2006).

of assessment evidence collected (specifically ability, creativity, and task commitment) but would allow them to select which assessment instruments to use during the identification process. Such differentiation would ensure a closer match between assessment instruments and the cultural backgrounds of those included in the campus talent pool. This consistent, yet flexible, identification process would open access to gifted and talented services for CLD students.

Impact on CLD Students: Linking the Gifted and Talented Interface Model and the GT Watch

A multipronged identification process can be represented on the "face" of the GT Watch, which provides a visual representation to the previously proposed gifted identification process with equal value given to ability, task commitment, and creativity. When plotting assessment data on the watch face, the results are the same, regardless of which assessment instrument is used. A child's individual results for each assessed area are plotted on a watch face by positioning the hands of the clock. Hence, the final "time" represents all of the assessment data collected during the identification process and indicates whether or not the child qualifies for gifted services. The same watch face can be used for any child at any campus, no matter how diverse.

If one truly believes that there are gifted and talented individuals in all cultures and populations, then gifted educators must adopt a more inclusive definition of giftedness. A wider net must be cast to include children from all cultural and ethnic backgrounds in the talent pool of potentially gifted, and all members of the talent pool should have equitable opportunities to demonstrate and develop individual areas of giftedness.

When considering CLD students, one must differentiate the identification process, such that the attributes that manifest giftedness or talent are not overlooked. Returning to the GT Watch metaphor, the basis for measuring the characteristics in a potential candidate is illustrated by the horizontal and vertical axes, as shown in Figure 3.8. This visualization is appropriate for the non-CLD candidate. One aspect of the multipronged identification of the CLD candidate is a differentiated perspective, which is represented by the modified faces in Figure 3.9. To continue with the watch metaphor, these differentiated faces represent varied economic, cultural, and linguistic identities and will be metaphorically referred to as CLD time zones.

For the non-CLD student, the traditional tools for entry into the gifted program should measure levels of ability, creativity, and task commitment. When considering an underrepresented CLD student, the perspective during the identification process must shift. The horizontal axis, signifying the norm

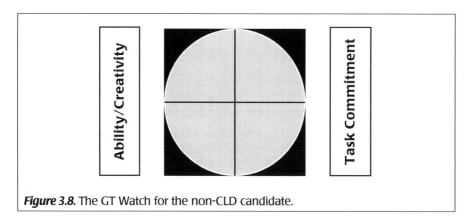

Figure 3.8. The GT Watch for the non-CLD candidate.

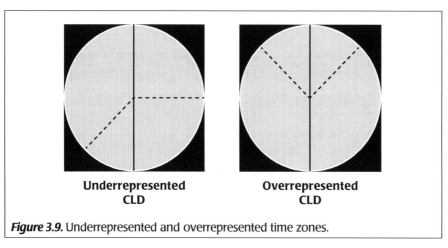

Underrepresented CLD

Overrepresented CLD

Figure 3.9. Underrepresented and overrepresented time zones.

or average ability/creativity according to traditional testing measures, must be widened to include attributes that may not be customarily considered. Such characteristics may include having a rich native language, high memory and observation skills, high analytical skills when examining relationships and people, ease of transfer of concepts from L1 to L2, sensitivity to varied perspectives, assuming leadership roles in the family, and keen sense of humor (Slocumb, 2006). The underrepresented CLD student may, even by traditional measures only, meet all criteria for entry into the program (the 12:00 or the 10:10 student). However, if an underrepresented student does not meet the minimum score for gifted entry on the traditional testing measures, the selection committee should consider the previously listed characteristics. This broader consideration is depicted in the underrepresented CLD time zone of the watch face.

The overrepresented CLD student is often selected for entry into the gifted program because of very high discipline levels, the emphasized cultural value to dedicate oneself to academic studies, the dedication set by the family to establish and meet goals, and the level of personal effort to strive for academic success. Although the overrepresented CLD student may meet the academic standards posed by traditional entry measures, the above-mentioned characteristics sometimes have an overshadowing effect. As a result, many 9:00 students, the overachievers (rather than true 12:00/10:10, or gifted, students), are represented in gifted programs. This is reflected in the overrepresented CLD time zone, where the horizontal axis is raised for both ability and task commitment.

Differentiated time zones capture attributes of cultural and linguistic diversity that may not otherwise be noticed using traditional non-CLD measures. A multipronged identification process that provides a menu of assessment instruments that value authentic thought and creativity using language neutral methods must be established. Educational environments should be purposefully designed to offer instructional and experiential opportunities to foster gifted potential. Such efforts would produce a larger talent pool of culturally and ethnically diverse individuals who demonstrate a need for gifted services. This philosophical shift directly opposes the traditional identification methods in which a few individuals are selected to participate in an assessment process that includes strict ability and/or achievement indicators and uses assessment instruments that are not language neutral, thereby favoring one cultural background over another. Shifting identification from the traditional exclusive approach of identification to an inclusive approach of serving *all* students exhibiting giftedness is the first step to transforming gifted education program services.

Chapter 4

Blending of Programs: Models and Design

The purpose of Chapter 4 is to elaborate upon the various gifted education program models that currently provide services to the identified gifted population and to present a comprehensive framework with blended program considerations for gifted education services.

Preview of Standard(s)/Term(s):

- ➻ *NAGC Standard 5.2. Coordinated Services*: Students with gifts and talents demonstrate progress as a result of the shared commitment and coordinated services of gifted education, general education, special education, and related professional services, such as school counselors, school psychologists, and social workers.
- ➻ *Program model*: The manner in which an identified student receives specialized services.
- ➻ *Co-teach*: Occurs when two licensed educators (not a teacher and a paraprofessional) with different areas of expertise preside over one or two classroom(s).
- ➻ *Team teach*: Occurs when two licensed educators (not a teacher and a paraprofessional) with similar areas of expertise preside over one or two classroom(s).
- ➻ *Subtractive bilingualism*: Linguistic process that seeks to build student proficiency in the target second language with decreased support in the first language.

➡ *Additive bilingualism*: Linguistic process that seeks to build student linguistic proficiency in both the native language and English.

Introduction

New approaches to identifying potential candidates for gifted and talented programs inevitably lead to the need for new program service designs that adequately serve CLD students. Other special instructional programs, such as bilingual education, English as a second language (ESL), and/or special education, may also serve qualifying students. Although such programs may seem disparate on the surface, they share many characteristics.

> Such commonalities call for a shift in thinking and no longer viewing these programs in isolation or mutually exclusive of the other.

Examining special programs, service models, and integration of best practices provides a broader perspective and understanding of the most effective instructional designs. Program services begin to be blended after the identification process is completed. This model, referred to as the Model of Blended Programs (MBP), synthesizes the structures of bilingual, ESL, special education, and gifted and talented programs to create both a comprehensive educational approach and an instructional delivery that best meet the needs of all students (see Chapter 5 for more information on this model).

Bilingual, ESL, special education, and gifted services are established based on mandates that ensure that every student has access to education and is being served in the most appropriate manner. Bilingual and ESL programs remove linguistic barriers that prevent full participation in public education. Through modified and accommodated instruction, special education programs also remove barriers that limit students' access to education. Although students in gifted and talented programs are not perceived to face any barriers to education, potentially gifted CLD candidates' failure to be properly identified for services suggests that qualified, yet unidentified, students are not being adequately served. Federal and/or state laws govern each of these programs through compliance procedures and guidelines concerning program implementation, such as identification procedures for program entry, accountability, funding, and adaptation of curriculum (see Figure 4.1).

The development of bilingual, ESL, and special education programs has been shaped by regulations and years of continuous research on the most effec-

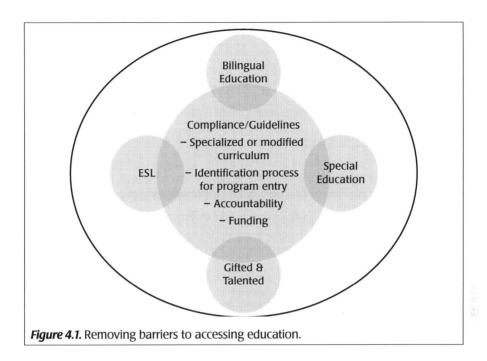

Figure 4.1. Removing barriers to accessing education.

tive ways to deliver such services. In 20 years of program evaluation research that culminated in their article, "The Astounding Effectiveness of Dual Language Education for All," Collier and Thomas (2004) concluded that dual language programs (where students receive academic instruction in English and a second language) and push-in models (where services are provided within the context of the classroom and are structured around the classroom activities) are the most effective bilingual and ESL programs, respectively. The reauthorization of IDEA in 2004, aligned with No Child Left Behind, called for full access to the general curriculum for special education students, leading to a strong inclination toward the inclusion model. Such research and program evaluations have led to the shift of pedagogical responsibility from one teacher (i.e., pull-out programs and self-contained classrooms) to a team-teach/co-teach model (i.e., dual language and inclusion) as a best practice for instructional delivery.

Blending of Programs: Program Models

Program model effectiveness is dependent on:
- ✔ the integrity of the model implementation,
- ✔ the competence of the educators to instruct within the model, and
- ✔ the capacity of the administrators to support the model.

The widespread team-teach/co-teach service delivery across bilingual, ESL, and special education disciplines raises the question of how such best practices can be blended into gifted program models. A closer examination of various grouping configurations in the context of each of these special programs is necessary to determine which would best suit the needs of culturally and linguistic diverse gifted students in a gifted program. Various factors should be considered to determine the most appropriate service delivery model for each local education agency. Table 4.1 illustrates the four most common programs and grouping configurations that address the instructional needs of each student group, for both elementary and secondary levels.

Gifted and Talented Program Models

Program models in gifted education are defined by the structure of services that are provided. At the elementary level, these services range from self-contained classrooms, to clustering identified gifted students within a general education classroom, to pull-out program services during the school day. At the secondary level, identified students have greater control in choosing from program services, which range from self-contained gifted courses, to clustering gifted students within Advanced Placement (AP) courses, to extracurricular activities designed to meet gifted students' educational needs. Within a gifted and talented program, there may be several models in operation. The program model may vary, but the *goals of service remain constant*. See Table 4.2 for an overview of gifted and talented programming models.

Many factors must be taken into consideration when determining the type of gifted education program model to be implemented. Some of those factors include:
- ➤ the number of students identified for gifted and talented services,
- ➤ the student demographics,
- ➤ the instructional and support personnel,
- ➤ the history of gifted and talented services provided in the school or district,
- ➤ the capacity of the program to meet gifted students' needs,

Table 4.1
Program Models and Components

Programs	Bilingual Education	Special Education		Gifted and Talented Education		English as a Second Language Education	
	Elementary (K–6)	Elementary (K–6)	Secondary (6–12)	Elementary (K–6)	Secondary (6–12)	Elementary (K–6)	Secondary (6–12)
Self-Contained * Class membership is all one program served by a program certified teacher.	X			X	X	X	X
Clustering Students are clustered in small groups within a general education classroom. The teacher is program certified.				X	X	X	X
Inclusion With Push-In Support Students remain in general education class but are not clustered with other identified students; program teacher comes into room for servicing.	X	X	X	X	X	X	X
Pull-Out Students are removed from the classroom content instruction.		X	X	X	X	X	X
Extended Learning Learning takes place outside the school day.				X	X		

*Special education students with qualifying disabilities may be served in a self-contained classroom.

Table 4.2
Gifted and Talented Program Models

Programs	Elementary	Secondary
Self-Contained Class membership is all gifted and talented students served by certified gifted education teacher.	X	X
Clustering Students are clustered in small groups within a general education classroom. The teacher is also certified in gifted education.	X	X
Co-Teach: Inclusion With Push-In Support Students remain in general education class but are not clustered with other identified students. The gifted education teacher comes into room for servicing.	X	X
Pull-Out Students are removed from the classroom content instruction.	X	X
Extended Learning Learning takes place outside the school day.	X	X

- the competence of the teaching staff serving in gifted education,
- the competence of the program administrators in gifted education, and
- the instructional resources available for gifted education.

Bilingual Program Models

In contrast to gifted and talented program models, the various bilingual program models define the goals of the program. Bilingual program models vary across states; transitional or dual language programs are the most prevalent, but the goals of each are distinct. A transitional bilingual program aims to utilize the L1 as a basis for gaining proficiency in L2. Over time, students' exposure to L1 decreases while their exposure to L2, the principal language for instruction and learning, increases. Because the goal is specifically to increase L2 proficiency at the expense of the L1, the transitional program model supports language learning through a *subtractive* process. In contrast, the dual language program model seeks to build both L1 and L2 proficiency, such that students become bilingual and biliterate. Because this program model develops L1 as well as L2, the dual language program model provides an *additive* instructional setting for language learning.

Within each of the bilingual program models, various grouping configurations may be established. Both transitional and dual language bilingual programs serve students through self-contained and co-teaching settings. The most appropriate setting depends on the availability of qualified personnel, the number of students identified for each program, and the chosen bilingual program model. See Table 4.3 for an overview of bilingual models and grouping configurations.

ESL Program Models

The most widely used ESL program models across the nation are either content-based or pull-out programs. Content-based ESL models provide English instruction through the lessons of academic subjects taught throughout the school day. This can be accomplished through a self-contained classroom, collaboration in a co-teaching configuration, or clustering within a general education classroom. In the pull-out model, ESL students are removed from the content-area instruction originally planned for the class in order to receive focused English instruction for a period of time. ESL students served under a pull-out model may or may not be physically removed from the classroom. See Table 4.4 for an overview of ESL programming models and grouping configurations.

Special Education Program Models

Current program models for special education are a direct result of legislation that calls for full access to the general education curriculum for those qualifying for special education services. Currently, inclusion models are commonly implemented at the elementary and secondary levels to achieve that full access. Although campus scheduling and staffing configurations are often complex, inclusion models can be simple in design. For example, at an elementary campus, a self-contained, grade-level teacher might co-teach with an inclusion teacher to plan and deliver instruction in all core subject areas. In contrast, at the secondary level, an inclusion teacher who specializes in a particular core content area may co-teach with several of the matching core content teachers at multiple grades. Program model considerations for special education services are primarily guided by the Individualized Education Program (IEP) for each student who qualifies for services.

Blending of Programs: Program Designs

Encapsulated within the program model is the program design. The program design refers to the components of a program model that are customized to meet the goals of the program, the needs of the individual classrooms, resources, program enrollment, logistics, and operations. Program design can

Table 4.3

Bilingual Program Models and Grouping Configurations

Programs	Transitional	Dual Language
Self-Contained Class membership is all one program served by a program certified teacher.	X	X
Co-Teach Students are served by two program certified teachers who collaborate to plan and deliver instruction.	X	X

Table 4.4

ESL Program Models and Grouping Configurations

Programs	Content-Based	Pull-Out
Self-Contained Class membership is all one program served by a program certified teacher.	X	
Co-Teach: Inclusion With Push-In Support Students are served by two program certified teachers who collaborate to plan and deliver instruction. Students remain in general education class but are not clustered with other identified students; program teacher comes into room for servicing.	X	
Clustering Students are clustered in small groups within a general education classroom. The teacher is program certified.	X	
Pull-Out Students are removed from classroom content-area lesson to receive focused instruction.		X

Table 4.5

Special Education Program Models and Grouping Configurations

Programs	Content-Based	Pull-Out
Self-Contained Class membership based on need demonstrated through psychological testing. Results indicate that educational need is more intense than can be addressed in a regular classroom setting. Service is all one program served by a program certified teacher.		X
Co-Teach: Inclusion With Push-In Support Students are served by two program certified teachers who collaborate to plan and deliver instruction. Students remain in the general education class but can be scheduled in same sections (secondary) with other identified students; program teacher comes into room for servicing.	X	

be modified in a multitude of ways, as illustrated by the Program Design Wheel shown in Figure 4.2.

As delineated in the previous section, gifted and talented, bilingual, ESL, and special education program models can use a wide range of grouping configurations. Students served under these programs may be grouped programmatically in a self-contained situation or be heterogeneously clustered with students in mainstream classes. Program designs also differ by subject area and language. For bilingual and ESL program models, each content area may be taught in a specific target language. In special education and gifted and talented programs, intentional accommodated instruction may be given in each subject area according to the student's individualized plan and area(s) of giftedness. Lastly, program designs could also differ according to scheduling, depending on the logistical operation of the school day and program. All four program types incorporate a minimum time period devoted to servicing the students. They are also limited to a maximum time period due to the operational constraints of the school day. In order to comply with minimum and maximum times, the rotation of classes could also be adjusted.

> Program Model Versus Program Design
> ✔ A *program model* is a structure that meets the instructional needs of a specific student population.
> ✔ *Program design* includes customized program components that meet the needs of the individual classrooms, resources, program enrollment, logistics, and operations.

The various program models define the goals of instruction. The way in which each of these goals is met depends on the program design, which is customized according to the needs of the students, resources, logistics, and operations of the school.

Table 4.6 shows a Rubric for Responsiveness, which provides a starting point for effectively assessing programs, determining whether program blending has been achieved, and evaluating whether components of a program are serving gifted and talented CLD students in a responsive manner. The rubric also indicates areas for improvement and development in anticipation of increased program responsiveness.

If the responses to the indicators shown in Table 4.6 are mostly *yes*, then the environment is ready for program change. If the responses are mostly *no* or *somewhat*, the activities directed at building capacity for change and collectively educating the program participants must begin in order for the program to be successful. If the responses are mixed, the areas of *no* and *somewhat* indicate

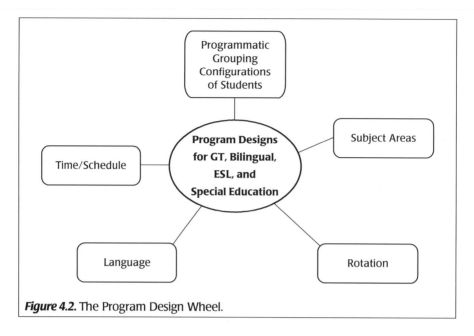

Figure 4.2. The Program Design Wheel.

where capacity building must begin. The importance of a complete and accurate examination of the program status cannot be overstated. It is imperative that a program self-assess in order to accurately develop and channel resources to the programmatic areas serving the students in greatest need. Evaluating current services is critical to programmatic development. The placement of the current services on a continuum provides additional insight into the responsiveness of the program to student services.

Table 4.7 elaborates the range of program responsiveness and provides indicators of service as a starting point for assessment. These indicators range from minimal to fully responsive, based on the activities demonstrated in each specific area. The rubric should be used to accurately assess current practices based on the indicators listed and to consciously adjust any components of the program that are not fully responsive.

Conclusion

By thoroughly examining the most effective program design components, administrators can synthesize programmatic pieces to achieve the most sophisticated levels of blending and better serve the particular instructional needs of gifted CLD students in a fully responsive manner.

Table 4.6
Rubric for Responsiveness

		Description	Yes	No	Somewhat
Program Model	Blending	Full integration of student programmatic services is provided in the classroom (some special education exceptions apply).			
Program Design	Blending	Incorporates all program services within the context of the classroom in order to provide services to the student in a holistic and authentic manner.			
	Coordination	Fully responsive program services are based on the student's needs and logistics for service are constructed based on those needs.			
	Communication	Communication levels between all service providers and the classroom teacher is continuous and student centered.			
Cultural	Instructional Materials	Instructional materials reflect the student populations' diversity. Teachers are encouraged to bring in outside resources exemplifying the various diverse cultures present in the student population.			
	Cross-Cultural Appreciation	Teachers are fully aware and well-versed in the diversity of their classroom and the cultures represented.			
		Celebrations and intentional incorporation of student cultures are a regular part of the curriculum.			
		Students are knowledgeable about all of the cultures in the classroom.			
	Value Added Diversity	Student identity and heritage are celebrated.			
		Acknowledgement of student identity and culture is authentic and provided through incorporation of real-world activities and student, family, and community sharing.			
Linguistic	Instructional Materials	Instructional materials are provided that reflect the native languages of the student population in all subject content areas.			
		Authentic literature is available and incorporated into instruction.			
	Second Language (L2) Appreciation	Linguistic comparative analysis is used frequently in acquiring English as a second language.			
		The native languages of the students are used as tools in learning and incorporated routinely as part of instruction.			
	Value-Added Diversity	Bilingualism is valued and continued linguistic growth in the native language is encouraged.			
		Student sharing of native language is incorporated routinely into the instruction.			

Table 4.7
Continuum for Program Responsiveness

		Minimal	Adequate	Fully Responsive
Program Model	**Program Model**			
	Blending	Few program services are integrated into the classroom. The delivery of program services is based on administrative ease, teacher preference, and outdated models of program services.	Some program services are integrated into the classroom while others are not addressed within the context of the classroom setting. Program service decisions are based on administrative ease, teacher preference, and/or logistics.	Full integration of student programmatic services is provided in the classroom (some special education exceptions apply). Integrated program service decisions are not based on administrative ease, teacher preference, or logistics
Program Design	**Program Design**			
	Blending	Program design does not integrate or designate specialized program services. All specialized services are delivered in isolation.	Some specialized program services are provided in the context of the classroom while other specialized services are delivered in isolation.	Incorporates all program services within the context of the classroom in order to service the student in a holistic and authentic manner.
	Coordination	No effort to coordinate or incorporate specialized services within the context of the classroom is provided.	Adequate program services consider the students' needs and logistics for service but do not necessarily structure delivery of services based on the students' best interests.	Fully responsive program services are based on the students' needs and logistics for service are constructed based on those needs.
	Communication	Little to no communication addressing student performance while receiving services is provided to the classroom teacher from the service provider.	Some communication between the service provider and classroom teacher is present.	Communication levels between all service providers and the classroom teacher is continuous and student centered.
Instructional Delivery				
	Instructional Materials	Instructional materials are not reflective of the student populations' diversity.	Some instructional materials reflect the student populations' diversity.	Instructional materials reflect the student populations' diversity. Teachers are encouraged to bring in outside resources exemplifying the various diverse cultures present in the student population.

Table 4.7, continued

Cultural	Cross-Cultural Appreciation	No encouragement, student sharing, or purposeful instruction is provided for cross-cultural appreciation.	Little attention is paid to celebrating and incorporating the various cultures into the classroom activities and studies.	Teachers are fully aware and well-versed in the diversity of their classroom and the cultures represented. Celebrations and intentional incorporation of student cultures are a regular part of the curriculum. Students are knowledgeable about all of the cultures in the classroom.
	Value-Added Diversity	Student heritage and cultural identity is not recognized or valued.	Acknowledgement of student identity and culture is given but no authentic exposure and sharing is demonstrated.	Student identity and heritage are celebrated. Acknowledgement of student identity and culture is authentic and provided through incorporation of real-world activities and student, family, and communities sharing.
Linguistic	Instructional Materials	Little to no materials are provided in the native languages of the student population.	Some materials are provided in the native languages of the student population. Use of authentic literature (not direct translations) is limited.	Instructional materials are provided that reflects the native languages of the student population in all subject content areas. Authentic literature is available and incorporated into instruction.
	Second Language (L2) Appreciation	No use of the student native language is incorporated into instruction.	Some linguistic, comparative analysis is incorporated into instruction. The students' native language is used as a springboard into acquiring English.	Linguistic comparative analysis is used frequently in acquiring English as a second language. The native languages of the students are used as an enrichment tool in learning and incorporated routinely as part of instruction.
	Value-Added Diversity	No benefit is recognized for being a second language learner.	Some recognition is given to the value of being bilingual and the support a second language provides in acquiring English, if practical.	Bilingualism is valued and continued linguistic growth in the native language is encouraged. Student sharing of students' native language is incorporated routinely into the instruction.

Section III:

Service Delivery

Chapter 5

Curriculum and Instruction

The purpose of Chapter 5 is to focus on best practices for instructing CLD students, with recommended extension activities to best serve gifted CLD students within the classroom context. Instructional differentiation and purposeful work for gifted CLD students are emphasized.

Preview of Standard(s)/Term(s):

➡ *NAGC Standard 3: Curriculum Planning and Instruction*: Educators apply the theory and research-based models of curriculum and instruction related to students with gifts and talents and respond to their needs by planning, selecting, adapting, and creating culturally relevant curriculum and by using a repertoire of evidence-based instructional strategies to ensure specific student outcomes.

➡ *Curricula*: Set of organized educational experiences that are developed by each core content area and are accepted by school professionals as essential for all students in the district.

➡ *Curriculum plan*: Adjusts core academic content to make it more meaningful to the child it serves.

➡ *Culturally relevant curriculum*: Builds upon the student's background knowledge, provides intentional, meaningful opportunities for student learning, and extends into the exploration and acquisition of cultural knowledge.

➻ *Culturally responsive curriculum*: Builds upon student strengths, interests, and background knowledge as it relates to the content being taught. Culturally responsive curriculum incorporates culturally relevant information and encompasses all aspects of diversity (e.g., cultural, linguistic) present in the classroom.

➻ *Level of service delivery* (I, II, III): Types of services provided to an identified gifted student with the varying levels based on the student's needs and area of giftedness.

➻ *Model of Blended Programs* (MBP): The integration of multiple special programs that work in collaboration to meet student educational needs. The MBP combines the most effective components of each special program into a single, comprehensive instructional approach in order to be truly responsive to the individual student's needs.

➻ *Instructional best practices*: Those strategies that make relevant connections between student knowledge and the information being learned in order to stimulate student learning.

➻ *Authentic literature*: Not a mere translation of English text, authentic literature provides a learning context in the student's first language and leads to the appreciation of heritage and maintenance of the primary language.

➻ *Authentic work*: A student-generated product resulting from authentic classroom learning; evidence of best practice instruction.

Introduction

The awesome responsibility of America's public schools is to provide a value-added educational experience to each student, each year, no matter the educational need. In addition, districts across the nation are obligated to design budgets that effectively meet the educational demands of students while maintaining the financial responsibility and integrity the community expects. A large part of a school system's operating budget is in the area of curriculum and instruction. Although curriculum and instruction tends to be well funded, too often the funding is earmarked or spread too thin to accomplish educational goals. Too frequently, federal and state resources provided to school districts are not sufficient to fully fund all educational programs; therefore, districts must look to outside resources for supplemental support. Often, such supplemental funds are temporary. In this time of economic unrest, repeated budget cuts, and increased educational accountability, educators must be innovative with the resources afforded to them.

School districts can no longer afford, and should no longer tolerate, a piecemeal approach to serving students. It is time for districts to efficiently and cost effectively reallocate resources. Reallocation starts by identifying the assets within each of the special program areas, purposefully blending those models and service designs, and providing qualified students with responsive, relevant, and high-quality educational services.

Model of Blended Programs

As discussed in Chapter 4, bilingual, ESL, special education, and gifted and talented programs have many common characteristics. The commonalities among these four traditionally separate programs demand a shift in organizational thought. No longer can programs that serve special populations be viewed as distinct, isolated models for service delivery. Instead, each should be considered a component of a dynamic Model of Blended Programs (MBP) that is fully integrated to meet each student's educational needs (see Figure 5.1). The MBP allows educators to combine the most effective components of each program to develop a curriculum that is truly responsive to the individual student the program serves. When considering how to serve the newly identified gifted CLD population, the notion of blended program and service delivery is especially critical.

The Gifted and Talented Interface Model (discussed in Chapters 2–3) used the metaphor of the GT Watch to illustrate a new definition of gifted and talented that was more inclusive of the CLD child. Each watch face represents areas of giftedness in a language neutral manner while recognizing that the level of task commitment can vary among the gifted. Regardless of the assessment tools a district uses to identify students for gifted and talented services, the GT Watch provides educators with a visual tool to symbolize this philosophical shift to a broader definition of gifted and talented. This new interpretation is desperately needed in the field of gifted education as it represents a more inclusive model of identification for nontraditional populations, specifically those that are culturally and linguistically diverse.

Without blending program models and service designs, the increased number of identified gifted CLD students could create a student population that is difficult to serve in a traditionally organized setting. However, once the program model type is identified and the level of cultural and linguistic responsiveness is determined (see Chapter 4), what remains is to design the most effective curriculum and service model for each qualifying student. It is this purposeful blending of programmatic resources that illustrates a more responsible educational and economic approach to service delivery.

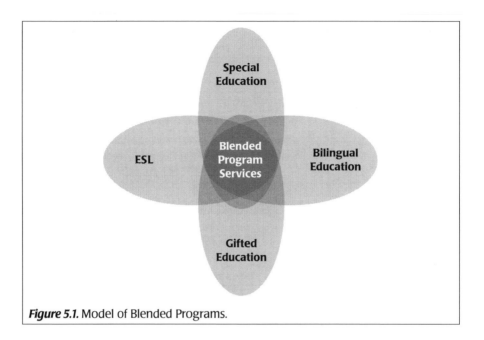

Figure 5.1. Model of Blended Programs.

Program Service = Curriculum + Instruction

Curriculum Development for Gifted CLD Students

Once identification practices more fully include CLD students, so must gifted curriculum and related services. Administrators, counselors, professionals with deep content knowledge and expertise in special program areas, and community members can collaborate in order to effectively combine resources to produce individually responsive curriculum.

Curriculum for the gifted and talented, especially gifted CLD students, should enrich the strengths of each child without creating academic gaps. A culturally responsive curriculum does not preclude a child from the basic foundations of the core curriculum, but instead allows each gifted child to explore and build upon those foundations using his or her strengths and interests. In their book, *Comprehensive Curriculum for Gifted Learners,* VanTassel-Baska and Stambaugh (2006) suggested that one of the first areas to address when assessing curriculum for the gifted is adapting the general curriculum within core areas to better respond to the atypical needs of the gifted student. A culturally relevant curriculum builds upon students' background knowledge, provides intentional, meaningful opportunities for student learning, and extends into the exploration and acquisition of cultural knowledge.

Curriculum Plan

It is reasonable to assume that not all gifted children, no matter what language they speak or their culture of origin, will be gifted in all core academic areas. Ability and achievement tests, coupled with student work samples, will help identify a child's general area of academic giftedness. Those areas may include, but are not limited to, strengths in verbal ability, quantitative ability, and/or other areas of critical thinking and reasoning. Once the area(s) to receive gifted services are determined, a curriculum plan is needed.

The curriculum plan modifies core academic content to make it meaningful to the student it serves. Modification can take the form of a variety of service models, including enrichment pull-out or push-in, acceleration, curriculum compacting, and/or other methods of differentiation that match the student's needs in a given situation. It is not necessary to rewrite the core curriculum for each content area. Instead, each core area should offer the gifted CLD student opportunities for self-directed learning experiences, utilizing the student's strengths as motivation to probe deep into the content, develop innovative ideas, ask new questions, make original connections, and think critically in order to make sense of these newly discovered ideas.

Curriculum planning at this level demands a collaborative approach between program experts, content specialists, and school administrators. Second language program experts contribute invaluable understanding of linguistic and cultural responsiveness as well as curriculum modifications that ensure the content is accessible through developmentally appropriate, linguistically accommodated instruction that matches the proficiency levels of the learner. Content experts contribute important knowledge specific to the core disciplines as well as conceptual considerations that are invaluable when promoting active research and inquiry.

Administrators provide the final, critical piece of the curriculum planning team. The administrator's knowledge of campus data, instructional goals, scheduling logistics, budgets, key personnel, and certifications is an important component of blending program services. Being included in curriculum planning provides administrators a deep understanding of content within the core academic disciplines and the modification opportunities for each. The natural consequence of this type of engagement is that administrators develop into instructional leaders, not simply building managers. Using a collaborative team approach to curriculum design builds a strong content structure and ensures that district-required student expectations are not compromised while gifted students learn and process content knowledge in ways unique to their educational needs.

It is imperative to gifted CLD children that curriculum design begins with the core content areas. This imperative becomes increasingly evident when examining the cause and effect relationship that occurs in the commonly practiced pull-out gifted service model.

Traditionally, in many places, gifted and talented services have been delivered via a pull-out approach where identified gifted students leave the regular classroom environment for enrichment lessons with a teacher certified in gifted education. Although such a service design may be effective for traditional, monolingual gifted children, the pull-out practice frequently puts gifted CLD students at greater risk for lower academic achievement. Essentially, a cause and effect relationship exists. When the traditional pull-out model is used to provide services to a gifted CLD student—"the cause" in the relationship—that student may frequently miss the introduction and/or practice of basic curriculum foundations, often in his or her first language. The pull-out model compromises the essential components for cognitive development: obtaining information in the first language to support the critical thinking needed to extend into the second language—the "effect" in the relationship. Hence, the commonly implemented pull-out approach has the potential to make long-term academic success more difficult for the nontraditional gifted student. Successful approaches to curriculum development for the gifted should include the proper adaptations needed to make the core curriculum more appropriate for the gifted learners it serves, in whatever setting it is delivered (VanTassel-Baska & Stambaugh, 2006).

In addition to curriculum development, there are other common components to consider when deciding how gifted services will be delivered. One component is the child's area(s) of identified giftedness. These areas could include, but are not limited to, academic disciplines.

A second component would be to determine the type of gifted service support needed. For example, could the student's giftedness be best developed in a mainstream classroom with differentiated instruction? If so, this would be considered a Level I type of support. If an independent study situation in which instruction may require acceleration or enrichment outside of what traditional differentiation can provide is necessary, a Level III type of service model would be necessary. A combination of Level I and Level III services might be most effective for a student. If so, the type of service required would meet in the middle at Level II.

The third component would be to determine how that support would be provided. If differentiation of core content in the regular classroom is sufficient, then the classroom teacher would provide the support. If the identified gifted child can benefit from support provided through differentiation, but perhaps needs enrichment in more than one area, then both the regular classroom teacher and the gifted specialist would deliver support. Finally, a child's need for gifted services may exceed what can happen in a regular classroom. If this is the case, then the gifted specialist would then be the one responsible for planning and facilitating experiences (e.g., independent study, mentorship programs), coordinating an acceleration plan, and encouraging participation in academic competitions or organizations that meet the needs of that particular student. This type of support would most likely require the student to continue to spend some time in the traditional classroom setting. Therefore, managing the communications between the gifted specialist and the classroom teacher would be crucial for the success of this type of gifted support.

Levels of Service

The following outlines the various types of service options and varying amounts of support that can be provided within the Model of Blended Programs:

I. *Differentiation within the regular classroom*: The teacher consults with the campus gifted specialist before planning differentiated lessons and activities based on the area of giftedness and social emotional needs. The gifted child is clustered with other Level I students in a regular classroom.

II. *Differentiation within the regular classroom with inclusionary services provided by the campus gifted specialist*: The teacher collaboratively develops and plans differentiated lessons and activities based on area(s) of giftedness and social-emotional needs with the campus gifted specialist; both have responsibility for facilitating classroom lessons. The gifted child is clustered with other Level II students in regular classroom.

III. *Differentiation happens both within the regular classroom with inclusionary services provided by the campus gifted specialist and outside the classroom with independent differentiation provided by the campus gifted specialist*: The teacher and gifted specialist collaboratively develop and plan differentiated lessons and activities based on area(s) of giftedness and social-emotional needs with the campus gifted specialist; both have responsibility for facilitating classroom lessons. The gifted child is clustered with other Level III (and possibly II) students in the regular classroom. At this level, the gifted student may be encouraged to explore interests via an independent study or self-paced approach.

Participation in such an independent learning situation would be mentored by the campus gifted specialist at the elementary levels and/ or a sponsor or community mentor at the upper grades.

Once the area of giftedness and level of service is determined for each child, an individual education service plan should be completed (see Figure 5.2). The education service plan follows the student throughout his or her school career and can be reviewed and modified as needed. The goal is to identify and deliver the most effective level of services for the student.

Additional Areas for Consideration

Services for gifted CLD students may also include nonacademic areas. As is common with other students receiving special services, gifted students also have social and emotional needs associated with their educational needs. As Silverman's (1997) research illustrated, gifted children's often asynchronous development requires unique social and emotional considerations throughout the formal educational years. Examples of this asynchronous development can easily be identified in physical development, peer relationships, perfectionism, organization, and leadership, to name a few. A counselor well versed in the attributes of the gifted population(s) identified and served on a campus or within a district is another integral component of a holistic gifted service model.

It is important for educators to understand that students who qualify for special services, especially gifted CLD children, bring unique counseling perspectives in the areas of physical, cognitive, social, and emotional development. Because of the nature of gifted and talented students' asynchronous development, common experiences in the classroom may produce anxiety for some students. For example, a gifted child who has perfectionist tendencies may experience great anxiety over missing a homework assignment or being given a time limit for completion. Another child may have brilliant intellect, but may become very nervous when asked to work with peers. In both cases, if there is not an awareness of the social and emotional needs of the gifted, students' reactions to these situations could be misinterpreted as unacceptable behaviors. Therefore, adding the services of a well-trained counselor and counseling staff to a blended program model for special populations is educationally, emotionally, and financially responsible. In a blended program response, the type of giftedness the student manifests determines the counselor's approach to serving the gifted student. The more knowledgeable and involved in the educational planning for the gifted students the counseling department becomes,

Gifted and Talented Education Service Plan

Student Name: _____ Grade: _____

Teacher: _____ Primary GT Contact: _____

Other professionals responsible for service delivery: _____

_____

School: _____

Date Services Begin: _____ Date Services Reviewed: _____

**Assessment data indicates student has qualified for services outlined in the following educational plan to address identified needs. **

Differentiated Service Level	Social-Emotional	Nonacademic area(s)	Area of Giftedness			
			Math	Science	ELA	SS
Level I: Differentiation w/in regular classroom						
Level II: Inclusionary support with co-teach model						
Level III: Inclusionary support coupled with self-paced, independent study						

Signature of Primary GT Contact: _____ Date: _____

Signature of General Education Teacher: _____ Date: _____

Signature of GT Counselor: _____ Date: _____

Signature of Campus Administrator: _____ Date: _____

Figure 5.2. Gifted and talented education service plan.

the more appropriate and complementary the support to the gifted students will be.

Finally, when serving gifted CLD students, a holistic approach to gifted and talented services must include a consideration of the arts, another area where a student's needs may be addressed in a more language neutral and culturally appreciative manner. The content and skills associated with an artistic area of interest can further develop and/or specifically address an area of giftedness, not only for gifted CLD students but also for gifted students with multiple exceptionalities, traditional gifted students, and/or those receiving a variety of other special services. Educators are presented with yet another opportunity to blend service models to make efficient, educationally responsible uses of resources afforded to administrators.

Instructional Delivery

Effective instructional delivery is defined by the ability to integrate the educational, social, and emotional needs of a student into the learning process. Best practice instruction is crucial when crafting an effective service design that honors the cultural identity of the student and considers linguistic diversity as an advantage in the learning process. To honor the requirements of a gifted CLD student's education service plan, all educators should be trained to teach to the strengths of the student and to value his or her contributions to the classroom environment.

Instructional best practices are most effective when a connection is made between the child and the information being learned. An effective teacher understands the power of getting to know her students and commits time throughout the year to study student data and create situations that build positive relationships within the classroom environment. As a part of getting to know one's students, many teachers send questionnaires home to parents to solicit information about their child's interests, hobbies, likes, dislikes, participation in afterschool activities, perceptions about school, and various other tidbits of general information (see Chapter 7). Parental input is vital when creating environments that are conducive to learning, feel safe for students, and encourage students to make connections between what they already know and what they are currently learning. Regardless of grade level, content studied, and/or special services being provided, it is in these types of situations where authentic learning takes place. It is in these safe environments that the identified gifted CLD child will develop academic capacity, but also where unidentified gifted CLD candidates will be given a chance to develop their academic potential.

Instructional best practices are made all the more relevant when the classroom environment clearly values the cultural contributions of all students. Teachers of gifted CLD students have many opportunities to highlight and incorporate cultural differences into instruction, which often results in both planned and unanticipated teachable moments. Teachable moments support the gifted CLD student by fostering cultural identity and creating a safe environment for taking academic risks.

The use of instructional materials and resources that represent the ethnic backgrounds exemplified by the student body demonstrates the commitment to including both direct and indirect culturally rich experiences into classroom instruction. Using authentic literature in the native languages of the students is one example of this commitment to being culturally responsive. Authentic literature is not translated from English texts but rather provides a learning context in the student's first language, which leads to the appreciation of heritage and maintenance of the primary language. When the cultural and linguistic diversity of the students is honored, fully responsive instructional delivery is realized. The result is a gifted CLD student whose cultural, linguistic, and affective needs are met, thereby enhancing the academic experience and producing a truly articulate, bilingual graduate who is able to think critically, creatively problem solve, and communicate effectively in a variety of real-life situations.

Authentic Work

Although a formal definition of authentic work has been debated and no formal consensus made, authentic work contains many valuable characteristics, the most important being that it is always unique to the student. Authentic work is a student-generated product that results from authentic classroom learning and provides evidence of best practice instruction. Obviously, this would exclude traditional worksheet-type activities, whether on paper or done with the use of expensive technology, as well as assessment tools that can be described as multiple choice, true/false, or fill in the blank. Educational artifacts provide educators with windows into the thoughts of students. More importantly, authentic work gives students a way to demonstrate understanding. In order to demonstrate understanding, a student must think. Thinking that requires a student to make connections between classroom learning and prior experiences, shows a student's perspective and insight of thought, and/or illustrates the connection between new and old information can all be represented with authentic work. Such work can take many forms in a classroom. It can be produced at all grade levels within any content area and provides all students an opportunity to demonstrate understanding without confining answers to any one structure or format.

It is important to note what types of traditional products cannot be categorized as authentic work. Because these products are unique to each student, authentic work cannot look like, or be defined as, any activity or assessment tool that requires a predetermined answer to be considered correct. As previously mentioned, this eliminates a true/false test, multiple-choice assessments, and a host of traditional types of activities and worksheets. Gone should be the days of classrooms and hallways adorned with colorful, decorative, symmetric bulletin boards that display teacher-purchased materials. Gone should be the days of classrooms and hallways filled with displays of work products that all look predictably similar because students were given the same assignment to complete. Gone should be the days when students are assessed based on a simple comprehension task at the end of a unit instead of on an essay requiring them to synthesize what they have learned. Present are the days when parents and administrators accept nothing less for children than dynamic learning environments where instructional best practices are the norm—environments that foster genuine learning as evidenced by products that represent each child's unique thoughts.

Such opportunities for students to demonstrate understanding are imperative to the identification of and service delivery to gifted CLD children. In a language neutral way, utilizing illustrations, graphic organizers, drama, manipulatives, and written expression in the primary language, authentic work products can provide educators with clues that gauge students' thought processes and abilities to process information, both as they move through each curriculum unit and grow academically throughout the year. As everyone in the class is given the opportunity to demonstrate the cognitive processes that illustrate ownership of learning, identified and potentially gifted CLD students will illustrate understanding in ways that set them apart from other students in the classroom.

A simple example of demonstrating understanding can be illustrated using the concept of addition, as shown by $4 + 5 = 9$. Traditional practice activities or assessments will look something like:

$$4 + \underline{\hspace{1cm}} = 9$$

or

$$9 = \underline{\hspace{1cm}} + \underline{\hspace{1cm}}$$

or

$$\underline{\hspace{1cm}} + 3 + \underline{\hspace{1cm}} = 9$$

Any child who has practiced number facts, used number flash cards, and/or participated in classroom instruction would most likely be able to demonstrate proficiency with this concept. However, when a student is given a blank piece of paper and asked to demonstrate his or her knowledge of the concept of addition by completing the following task, the possible responses are endless:

Represent or illustrate the way numbers can be used to total 9.

Student A: A typical response would be an illustration of some type of grouping of items to show 9.

Student B: A more advanced response might include an illustration like that in the basic response labeled with the mathematical equation. By demonstrating the concept of grouping to accomplish 9 in three different ways, Student B shows a deeper level of understanding than Student A.

$$4 + 5 = 9 \qquad 3 + 6 = 9 \qquad 1 + 8 = 9$$

Student C: A response that shows ownership of learning may include what Students A and B have done, but might also demonstrate knowledge of fractions or decimals:

$$4\ 1/2 + 4\ 1/2 = 9$$
$$\text{or}$$
$$4.6 + 4.4 = 9$$

Of the three students, it is obvious that Student C clearly has the deepest conceptual knowledge of addition and the various ways in which numbers can be used as whole or parts to equal the sum of 9. All three of the above pieces are examples of authentic work because the student was given an open-ended task and asked to demonstrate his or her personal understanding. There were no boundaries; each student was required to show in his own way that he understood the concept of addition.

Conclusion

With newly revamped identification procedures that are more inclusive of CLD students, it is imperative that the demographic makeup of a campus, teacher and administrator competency, and level of program support are carefully considered when designing a gifted program model. Such considerations must begin with an honest, critical evaluation of the current program model and service design, using the previously presented set of rubrics outlined in Chapter 4. Once implemented, the Rubric for Responsiveness (Table 4.6) must match the needs of the students whom the model will serve in order to be categorized as fully responsive.

In addition, administrators must take careful inventory of the available resources—both personnel and materials, on campus and within the district—to be educationally and financially responsible to the community their schools serve. The Model of Blended Programs encourages the efficient use of resources.

Finally, curriculum and instructional best practices must work in concert to create a culturally responsive environment and relevant curriculum that includes opportunities for meaningful learning. Ownership of learning should look different for each student, as each student makes meaning in discrete, individual ways. Evidence of such ownership comes from best practice instruction that assigns meaningful work and results in authentic work samples. Using authentic work as best practice allows gifted potential to develop and honors the perspectives and insights associated with giftedness. It is in this dynamic environment that truly effective gifted education services will be provided to culturally and linguistically diverse students.

Chapter 6

Professional Development

Chapter 6 presents a model for working with and supporting teachers through a professional development framework. Baseline competencies and a matrix for professional self-assessment for CLD gifted educators will be articulated.

Preview of Term(s):

➤ *Baseline competencies*: Foundational knowledge and skills necessary to develop abilities, strategies, and aptitude for effective instruction.

➤ *Professional preparation*: The process of aligning the educator's skill set with the necessary knowledge and skills for serving culturally and linguistically diverse students.

➤ *Professional collaboration*: Partnership and cooperation with other educators at the team, campus, and district levels and beyond.

➤ *Professional development*: One's own acquisition of knowledge, either through formal classes or training and field experience.

Campus-based gifted and talented program educators, campus administrators, and district program support personnel strive to address the needs of gifted learners within the district program model. In order to be fully responsive to the needs of each gifted learner, districts must put into place professional preparation structures that support program models, service designs, and gifted and talented program educators. Responding to the professional needs of educators requires thoughtful planning and implementation of a professional preparation model. Professional development allows a campus or district to transform current practices into ones that incorporate the needs of a changing student demographic and a culturally and linguistically diverse gifted population.

Utilizing professional collaboration and professional development to reach a level of expertise to effectively serve the gifted CLD student is an individualized process. Landrum, Callahan, and Shaklee (2001) asserted that school staff should "enter and exit the enduring cycle of professional development activity based on previous knowledge and experience and the need for information as it relates to their professional role in the education of gifted learners" (p. 68). Educators of gifted CLD students should determine their acquired knowledge of providing gifted education services for these students, establish professional goals, and formulate a plan of action to reach those goals. Because each educator's level of knowledge and goals is distinct, such a plan of action must be individualized. Furthermore, the process should include opportunities to acquire the necessary knowledge and skills and guidance in becoming leaders within their own campuses and districts.

The 4P Framework: Personalized Professional Preparation Plan

In order to facilitate the professional learning endeavors, the 4P Framework has been developed by the authors. The 4P Framework organizes the process of reaching professional goals based on each educator's current knowledge, strengths, and skill sets and is customized to meet the individual educator's professional growth needs. The available course of action and opportunities to meet those needs are aligned to the district's overall goals and vision. The overall purpose of the framework is to equip novice teachers with the necessary skills and knowledge to build capacity from within and to grow them into leaders of gifted CLD education.

Developing Baseline Competencies as a Gifted CLD Educator

There is a certain amount of basic knowledge that the gifted CLD educator needs as a foundation upon which to build instructional competency. Such baseline competencies cover foundational principles, instructional strategies, and research-based best practices in the areas of gifted and talented education as well as cultural and linguistic diversity (see Figure 6.1).

Basic gifted and talented education courses should impart knowledge and understanding of the characteristics, needs, identification, and assessment of

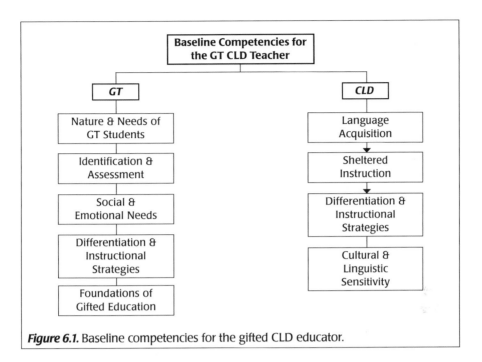

Figure 6.1. Baseline competencies for the gifted CLD educator.

gifted and talented students. Such professional development should discuss foundational theories and research in the field as well as instructional strategies and differentiated curriculum.

The complementary course of study for gifted educators serving CLD students addresses cultural and linguistic diversity. A firm grasp on language acquisition research and sheltered instruction methodology is imperative for serving CLD students. The arrows in Figure 6.1 depict the sequential nature of these two topics. Thereafter, professional development in differentiation, instructional strategies, sensitivity, and building awareness of the characteristics and needs of CLD students should be acquired.

Baseline competencies can be acquired through university coursework, professional organizations, service centers, education agencies, and/or school districts. Depending on the opportunities for professional development and training, some topics may be more available than others. Although such pacing is left to the discretion of each teacher or bound to local or state requirements, effective gifted CLD educators are aware of their levels of expertise and skills in these specific areas and respond accordingly to meet their professional goals.

Self-Assessment of Professional Preparation

In order to effectively meet the needs of a changing student demographic, educators must align their professional knowledge, strengths, and skill sets to the identified student need. The first step in this process is to measure one's current professional training with a self-assessment. The Matrix for Professional Preparation: A Self-Assessment (see Table 6.1) may be utilized to reveal professional strengths as well as areas of needed improvement. Areas of professional preparation are further categorized into professional collaboration and professional development.

Professional collaboration refers to partnership and cooperation with other educators at the team, campus, and district levels and beyond. This collaboration can be structured or less formal. Ideas include networking at conferences, participating in staff sharing sessions and reflections, attending retreats and brown-bag lunches, observing each other's classes, presenting at conferences or meetings, fostering coaching relationships, building cadres/committees, and visiting other classrooms or sites (Imbeau, 2006). Professional development refers to one's own acquisition of knowledge through classes, workshops, training, and field experience. Such knowledge and skills could also be gained through enrolling in online courses, attending conferences, completing graduate coursework, attending institutes or academies, or performing research (Imbeau, 2006).

Based on the analysis of their current professional preparation and student, campus, and district programmatic priorities, educators can establish goals each year to advance in one or more areas. The successful acquisition of baseline competencies serves as the starting point for professional growth as a gifted education teacher serving CLD students. Once goals are determined, an action plan to reach those levels may be implemented.

After completing self-assessments, gifted CLD educators should have an overview of where they stand in their professional preparation, the first step in establishing goals for the year. Figure 6.2, the 4P Pyramid, suggests a level of preparation for each year as a gifted CLD educator. Note that the years listed in the pyramid are fluid and may not reflect each individual's current standing according to the self-assessment. Educators should focus on the stage and levels at which they find themselves.

In the first and second years of service, the gifted CLD educator has the opportunity to develop baseline competencies that will serve as a foundation upon which to build solid instruction. During this time, the educator also acquires experience serving gifted CLD students and benefits from the support of a mentor. The third, fourth, and fifth years mark a transitional period in which the teacher has experience serving gifted CLD students, shows competency in best practices and instructional strategies, and yields student success. In the transitional period, the teacher also begins to assume leadership roles by supporting novice teachers or participating in committees and/or organiza-

Table 6.1

Matrix for Professional Preparation: A Self-Assessment

Area of Professionalism	Professional Collaboration			
	Novice		**Transitional**	**Mentor**
Mentorship	I am a mentee who regularly meets with my mentor. I need this partnership to be an effective teacher.	I am a mentee, but not dependent on my mentor to be effective.	I am a mentor who may meet with my mentee, but does not significantly contribute to his or her effectiveness.	I am a mentor who regularly meets with my mentee and contributes to his or her effectiveness as an educator.
Professional Learning Communities (PLCs)	I do not participate in regular PLCs or collaborate with other educators who are gifted CLD educators.	I collaborate with others on gifted/CLD topics, but not in a PLC environment.	I attend PLCs with others on gifted CLD education.	I assume leadership roles in PLCs on a regular basis, addressing gifted/CLD topics.
Campus/District Orientation	I do not participate in campus policies and decisions regarding gifted CLD students, program development, and policy.	I participate in campus policies and decisions regarding gifted CLD students, program development, and policy.	I assume leadership roles in campus policies and decisions regarding gifted CLD students, program development, and policy.	I assume leadership roles in district policies and decisions regarding gifted CLD students, program development, and policy.
Committee or Organizational Membership	I am not a member of any district or school committee and/or a professional organization that incorporates gifted CLD student issues.	I am an inactive member of any district or school committee and/or a professional organization that incorporates gifted CLD student issues.	I am an active member of a district or school committee and/or a professional organization that incorporates gifted CLD student issues.	I assume leadership roles in a district or school committee and/or a professional organization that incorporates gifted CLD student issues.

Area of Professionalism	Professional Development			
	Novice		**Transitional**	**Mentor**
Gifted Baseline Competencies	I have not completed any requirements to be qualified as a gifted teacher.	I have completed some requirements to be qualified as a gifted teacher.	I have completed all requirements to be qualified as a gifted teacher.	I assume leadership roles on teaching baseline competency topics.
CLD Baseline Competencies	I have not completed any professional development.	I have completed some professional development.	I have completed all baseline competency recommendations. I hold ESL and/or bilingual certification.	I assume leadership roles on baseline competency topics.
CLD Experience	I have not had full-time classroom experience serving CLD students.	I have had 1–2 years of full-time classroom experience serving CLD students.	I have had 3+ years of full-time classroom experience serving CLD students.	I have had 3+ years of full-time classroom experience serving CLD students.
Gifted Experience	I have not had full-time classroom experience serving gifted students.	I have had 1–2 years of full-time classroom experience serving gifted students.	I have had 3+ years of full-time classroom experience serving gifted students.	I have had 3+ years of full-time classroom experience serving gifted students.
Continuing Education	I have not completed any coursework or professional development beyond the baseline competencies.	I attend workshops or training on gifted and CLD topics.	I am pursuing an advanced degree in the area of GT and/or CLD education.	I am pursuing an advanced degree in the area of GT and/or CLD education.

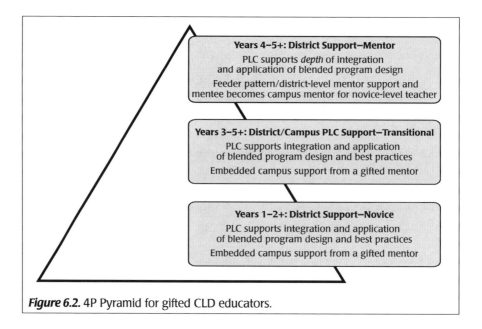

Figure 6.2. 4P Pyramid for gifted CLD educators.

tions at the campus, district, or community level(s). After the individual has surpassed the transitional period, he or she may continue to assume greater responsibilities and leadership roles, serving as an official mentor and facilitating the process to help others to reach this level as well.

Similar to the 4P Pyramid for gifted CLD educators, the 4P Pyramid for administrators is structured to reflect the same progression of novice educators into leadership (see Figure 6.3). During the first and second years of service, administrators of gifted classes and programs that include CLD students must develop the same baseline competencies as teachers. It is necessary for these administrators to be well-versed in gifted education and sheltered instruction and demonstrate sensitivity to cultural and linguistic diversity. Administrators who are competent in these areas are able to support teachers and parents and promote a school environment that values gifted CLD students. Simultaneously, the novice administrator also benefits from a mentoring administrator who has experience successfully building and leading his or her own gifted programs that serve CLD students. At the transitional stage, the administrator has gained experience and knowledge and begins to plan and build professional learning communities that provide opportunities for teachers and support personnel to participate in district-level programming support. Finally, the administrator assumes greater leadership positions, becoming a mentor to new campus administrators who are leading gifted programs serving CLD students as well as a mentor to teachers.

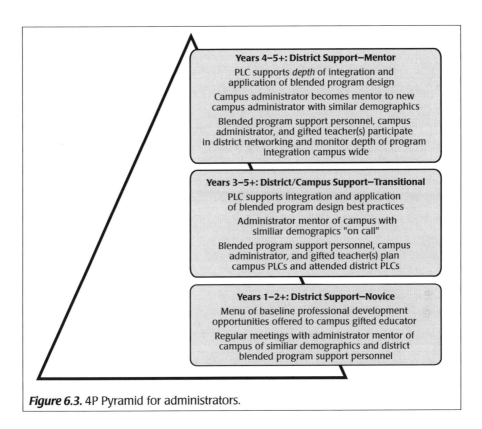

Figure 6.3. 4P Pyramid for administrators.

Utilizing the 4P

Once the self-assessment has been completed and the gifted CLD educator has gained an understanding of his or her current stage of novice, transitional, or mentor, a course of action through the 4P should be made. The individual should set professional collaboration and professional development goals, identify professional activities to meet the established goals, and thereby progress to the next stage in each area by the end of the school year.

The 4P documents the competencies of the teacher in her respective plan and provides a learning continuum to guide her in the acquisition of knowledge and professional growth. This prioritizes obtaining the basic knowledge and skills to serve gifted CLD students. The results of the self-assessment are also recorded on the 4P so that the goals for the year can be solidified. The individual should, at minimum, create two goals for two different subcategories of professional collaboration and two goals for two different subcategories for professional development for the school year. The activities to meet each of those goals should ideally help the individual to progress to the next stage of the 4P Pyramid by the end of the year. The chosen activities should be measureable and quantified, if necessary, and the timeline should indicate if the activity is an ongoing action throughout the year or a one-time event. The end-of-the-year examination revisits the 4P and ascertains if the goals for the year have been met. Based on the goals, the individual may or may not advance in his or her stage according to the 4P Pyramid.

To facilitate these professional activities, templates are provided in Figure 6.4 for a professional plan, a self-assessment, and goals and course of action for professional development. The review of baseline competencies ensures that foundational knowledge in both gifted and talented education as well as second language acquisition is established. The results of the self-assessment matrix provide a context for which professional objectives may be determined. This comprehensive and intentional approach allows for substantive reflection and planning to channel meaningful professional collaboration and development toward a focused goal.

Personalized Professional Preparation Plan (4P) for Educators of Gifted CLD Students

20___ –20___ School Year

Name: _____ School: _____

Position: _____ Grade level(s): _____

Number of completed years in current position/grade level: _____

Number of completed years serving CLD students: _____

Number of completed years of educational experience: _____

Number of completed years serving GT students: _____

A Review of Baseline Competencies

Gifted and Talented Competencies	Culturally and Linguistically Diverse Competencies
Indicate which gifted baseline competencies you have acquired, how, and the dates they were completed: ____ Gifted state certification (Date: _____) How: ____ ____ Gifted clock hours (initial) (Date: _____) How: ____ ____ Gifted university coursework (Date: _____) How: ____	Indicate which CLD baseline competencies you have acquired, how, and dates they were completed: ____ Second language acquisition (Date: _____) How: ____ ____ Sheltered instruction (Date: _____) How: ____ ____ Differentiation and instructional strategies (Date: _____) How: ____ ____ Cultural and linguistic sensitivity (Date: _____) How: ____

Results of a Matrix for Professional Preparation: A Self-Assessment

Professional Collaboration			Professional Development		
Please circle to indicate the results of the self-assessment in each subcategory:			Please circle to indicate the results of the self-assessment in each subcategory:		
Mentorship:	Novice	Transitional	Mentor	Gifted Baseline Competencies: Novice	Transitional	Mentor
PLCs:	Novice	Transitional	Mentor	CLD Baseline Competencies: Novice	Transitional	Mentor
Campus/District Orientation:	Novice	Transitional	Mentor	CLD Experience: Novice	Transitional	Mentor
Committee Membership:	Novice	Transitional	Mentor	Gifted Experience: Novice	Transitional	Mentor
				Continuing Education: Novice	Transitional	Mentor

Figure 6.4. Templates for a personal professional plan, self-assessment, and goals and course of action.

Stage of 4P Pyramid

Based on the 4P Pyramid, my overall stage of professional collaboration is:	Novice	Transitional	Mentor
Based on the 4P Pyramid, my overall stage of professional development is:	Novice	Transitional	Mentor

Goals and Course of Action for Professional Collaboration

Goal #1:			Activities to meet goal:	Timeline:	Date Completed:
Mentorship:	Novice	Transitional	Mentor	a.		
PLCs:	Novice	Transitional	Mentor			
Campus/District Orientation:	Novice	Transitional	Mentor	b.		
Committee Membership:	Novice	Transitional	Mentor	c.		

Goal #2:						
Mentorship:	Novice	Transitional	Mentor	a.		
PLCs:	Novice	Transitional	Mentor			
Campus/District Orientation:	Novice	Transitional	Mentor	b.		
Committee Membership:	Novice	Transitional	Mentor	c.		

Goals and Course of Action for Professional Development

Goal #1:			Activities to meet goal:	Timeline:	Date Completed:
GT Baseline Competencies:	Novice	Transitional	Mentor	a.		
CLD Baseline Competencies:	Novice	Transitional	Mentor			
CLD Experience:	Novice	Transitional	Mentor	b.		
Gifted Experience:	Novice	Transitional	Mentor	c.		
Continuing Education:	Novice	Transitional	Mentor			

Figure 6.4., continued

Goal #2:

				a.
GT Baseline Competencies:	Novice	Transitional	Mentor	
CLD Baseline Competencies:	Novice	Transitional	Mentor	b.
CLD Experience:	Novice	Transitional	Mentor	
Gifted Experience:	Novice	Transitional	Mentor	c.
Continuing Education:	Novice	Transitional	Mentor	

End-of-Year Examination of Goals

Professional Collaboration			Professional Development		
Goal #1 met?	Yes	No	Goal #1 met?	Yes	No
Goal #2 met?	Yes	No	Goal #2 met?	Yes	No

Based on the 4P Pyramid, my overall stage of professional collaboration is now: Novice   Transitional   Mentor

Based on the 4P Pyramid, my overall stage of professional development is now: Novice   Transitional   Mentor

Date 4P initiated (beginning of year): _____   Date 4P completed (end of year): _____

Signature of individual: _____

Figure 6.4., continued

Chapter 7

Family and Community

The purpose of Chapter 7 is to build the understanding that successful gifted programs serve not only gifted and talented students, but also families and communities. Strategies for building community support will be elaborated, and strategies for working with cultural and linguistically diverse students will be discussed.

Preview of Standard(s)/Term(s):

↠ *NAGC Programming Standard 4*: Learning environments foster personal and social responsibility, multicultural competence, and interpersonal and technical communication skills for leadership in the 21st century to ensure specific student outcomes.

↠ *NAGC Programming Standard 5*: Educators are aware of empirical evidence regarding (a) the cognitive, creative, and affective development of learners with gifts and talents, and (b) programming that meets their concomitant needs. Educators use this expertise systemically and collaboratively to develop, implement, and effectively manage comprehensive services for students with a variety of gifts and talents to ensure specific student outcomes.

↠ *Parental question stems*: Open-ended questions that prompt for exploration in communication and reflective thought in the response without guiding the response.

Introduction

The seamless integration of family and community support is a hallmark of exemplary gifted and talented programs. Before such support for gifted and talented education can be garnered within the school community, a common understanding of what giftedness is and who gifted students are must be established. A true partnership between school and family/community rests upon a firm foundation consisting of awareness of gifted and talented education and appreciation for the extraordinary characteristics of gifted children, whose effort and abilities can be channeled into remarkable outcomes that benefit both their families and communities.

Establishing a common appreciation and understanding for giftedness among diverse cultures is not an easy task. Giftedness is typically perceived as a positive trait by mainstream American society but this is not necessarily a view shared by everyone. When considering the gifted culturally and linguistically diverse student, educators must realize that the degree of reverence for, and therefore priority of, gifted and talented services is not necessarily globally viewed with the same perspective.

> Consider 5-year-old Carlos, who possesses a high level of cognitive competence, musical talent, highly developed verbal skills, keen sense of humor, and mature reasoning skills. When his parents, who recently immigrated to the U.S., are delivered the exciting news from his teacher that their son has strong potential to be placed in the gifted and talented program, they cannot hide their quizzical look that borders on anxiousness. They respond, "What does that mean? What is a gifted and talented program? We don't want our child to be abnormal—we want him to have a normal, happy life."

> Consider 8-year-old Taylor, whose 99th percentile score on a norm-referenced achievement test, unwavering discipline, and meticulousness make her an ideal candidate for the gifted and talented services. Upon notice of acceptance into the program, her proud parents immediately congratulate her and spread the good news to their family and friends. She is destined to have a bright scholastic future, just as her parents did.

> Lastly, consider 9-year-old Mi-Kyung, who immigrated to the U.S. with her parents just 2 years ago. Her grades and achieve-

ments are unrivaled by both former students and present classmates. Mi-Kyung's academic abilities and musical talent surpass every expectation that her teachers have of her. When given the news that their child has extraordinary abilities that would place her into the gifted and talented program, her parents are unmoved and not surprised. In response to the news, Mi-Kyung's parents ask the teacher if there is extra work or additional skills she can hone on the weekends and after school.

Each of the above scenarios depicts a different cultural perception and value of giftedness. The response of each of the parents is commensurate with their background knowledge of gifted and talented programs, which is directly tied to their home cultures. In Taylor's case, her parents' excitement implies an appreciation for giftedness. Having completed their education through the U.S. school system, they understand that only a small percentage of students qualify for gifted and talented services. In a study conducted by Okagaki and Sternberg (1993), Latino Americans were found to emphasize and promote the development of socioemotional competence, while Asian Americans emphasized cognitive competence. This idea is illustrated in the cases of Carlos and Mi-Kyung, which represent varying degrees of value and appreciation placed on giftedness. For Carlos's parents, it is important for him to do well in school, but they are unsure of what being gifted implies for him. Their lack of familiarity with gifted and talented programs indicates an absence or rarity of such identification and services in their home country. This unfamiliarity prompts them to question whether this new label would affect him or his childhood negatively. Mi-Kyung's parents truly value their child being identified as gifted. However, their appreciation for what others may consider a prestigious and rare occurrence is somewhat minimized due to their expectations. In Mi-Kyung's home country, academic excellence and high achievement throughout one's school career are the best indicators of a secure future. Being academically gifted is not extraordinary—it is the standard.

Given these incongruent cultural perceptions of gifted and talented programs, schools and districts must establish both a common understanding of and an appreciation for giftedness in order to gain family and community support. Educating families about gifted identification and delivering subsequent services are most effective when schools strive to connect both culturally and linguistically with parents. Parents whose cultural and linguistic needs are honored and met are more likely to understand and support their gifted children as well as gifted programs.

Parent and family involvement in gifted programs varies. Initially, parents may be involved in the student identification and qualification process. Oftentimes, parents are notified that their child has been considered for the gifted program and that they will need to complete paperwork that will play a role in the overall qualification process for the student. Parents who are not familiar with gifted programs are often unaware of the weight their responses may carry or even unsure if such a program will benefit their child. To bridge this gap, schools should provide informational meetings conducted in a style that connects with families of potentially gifted students who are culturally and linguistically diverse. In order to accomplish such a connection, schools must be aware of and sensitive to the cultural needs and linguistic diversity of families. Table 7.1 describes various strategies to meet these needs.

Schools that reach out to and successfully connect with parents, especially those of gifted CLD students, will reap more accurate results throughout the qualification process, more support for the program, and greater collaboration between home and school.

Once parents understand gifted student characteristics and how the gifted program meets these students' needs, a partnership between home and school must be created to link gifted students, teachers, and families. Best instruction and true authentic learning always reflects a partnership between school and home. When the school day or year ends, it is the parents' responsibility to provide their child with extension opportunities that expand on whatever interests classroom instruction prompted. Gifted behaviors do not stop when the bell rings at 3:15, but instead flow continuously into the home environment. Ideally, such learning extensions would happen in every home after school hours. The reality is that this just doesn't happen. Therefore, capitalizing on student interests, providing those extension opportunities, and connecting classroom learning to the outside world are critical best practices for meeting the needs of the gifted CLD student.

The teacher plays a vital role in establishing the home-school connection. Because parents do not always know how to support their child's learning from school, they also need to be taught how to recognize the specific needs of their gifted child. Table 7.2 provides a series of question stems that may be provided to the parents in order to garner information about the student's needs.

At the root of the reciprocal relationship between school, home, and community, it is imperative to have common understanding, effective communication, and trust. As discussed above, all stakeholders must share a consistent understanding of the definition of gifted and talented, its programmatic purpose (how it will meet the educational needs of CLD students), and its benefit (how the education of gifted CLD students will benefit the community). Providing

Table 7.1

Meeting the Cultural and Linguistic Needs of Parents

Meeting Cultural Needs of Parents	Meeting Linguistic Needs of Parents
Research the level of familiarity with gifted programs by represented cultural groups. Based on this information, build awareness about gifted programs, characteristics of gifted students, the qualification process, and areas of qualification. Describe benefits and need of providing gifted programs.	If the person who is conducting the meeting is unable to deliver the information in the parents' native language, provide an interpreter.
Always greet parents warmly and ensure them that they are a valuable part of the identification process as well as a partner in the education of their child.	Provide all forms and questionnaires in parents' native language. Review these forms and questionnaires using less formal language so that parents are clear on what is being asked.
Research cultural expectations of students of represented cultural groups. Build awareness of gifted students' needs, both academic and emotional, and how parents can support or meet these needs in the home.	Create an environment (which may be less formal than usual parent meetings) that allows parents to discuss and ask questions or express concerns.
Research the value that the represented culture groups place on specific talents and gifts. Inform parents on how to recognize gifted behaviors and characteristics that may not be as valued in their cultures.	Avoid using language that is too technical or specific to education that noneducators may not understand. Keep any printed material simple and clear and provide definitions when needed.

material to help parents identify gifted behaviors witnessed in the home serves two purposes. First, the questions enhance overall understanding of giftedness and provide possible reasons for patterns of behaviors demonstrated by their child. Second, the questions help facilitate a collaborative, trusting dialogue between the home and school that is valuable not only when identifying CLD students with gifted and talented potential, but also when designing their subsequent learning environments. With NAGC Programming Standard 4.5.2, the educator is charged with providing opportunities and resources that recognize a student's cultural context and further support the student's enhanced academic, social-emotional, and cultural competence. Ideally, the structure of the classroom within a gifted program would reflect a pluralistic, diverse society, allowing students to develop in the confidence of their culture and the competence of others.

Home

Effective communication starts with establishing and nurturing a mutual trust between the stakeholders. Trust comes when all of those involved truly listen to the information that each provides and use it for the educational bet-

Table 7.2
Question Stems for Parents

General
• What interests has your child had that have spanned over long periods of time?
• Would you describe those interests as a "phase?" Why or why not?
• Does your child set goals for him- or herself? If so, can you share some examples?
• Are those goals achieved? If so, what happens next? If not, are the goals abandoned or just still "in the works"?
• In what ways does your child use his or her imagination?
• How would you describe your child's quality of work at home?
• How would you describe your child's behavior at home?

Social/Emotional
• On a scale of 1–10, with 1 being low and 10 being high, how would you describe your child's self-confidence?
• Would you describe your child as a leader? Why or why not? Please provide examples.
• Is he or she confident in new situations?
• How does your child adapt to those situations?
• How does your child make friends?
• How would you describe your child's expectations for him- or herself?

Study Skills
• How does your child manage his or her time?
• Is that same pattern followed at school and home?
• Is your child self-motivated? Why or why not? Provide examples.

Information Gathering
• What is your child's attitude about learning?
• Is the attitude consistent among all academic areas or is there an area or two than may be different from the others? Explain.
• At what pace does your child learn factual information?
• Is that information retained immediately or after some practice? Give examples.
• How would you describe your child's vocabulary?
• How would you describe your child's insight on areas that interest him or her?
• How does your child approach asking questions?

terment of the student. For example, consider the answers to the parent questions stems. If educators sincerely listen with a culturally neutral ear, the parent responses open insightful windows into the minds and behaviors of the gifted CLD child. Educators can use the parental feedback to watch more closely how the child learns and interacts with others and to authentically communicate those observations to parents.

Furthermore, because establishing trust and a common understanding among stakeholders is an ongoing and a reciprocal process, parents can also glean important information by listening to the feedback provided by their child's teacher. Parents are then afforded the opportunity to naturally extend classroom learning into the home. Therefore, just as educators gain insight from parent responses, such as those listed in Table 7.3, parents can also deepen their

Table 7.3.

Feedback That Can Be Provided by Teachers

General
<ul><li>It's been observed that you child often chooses to read books about _____ and/or write about _____. This has continued throughout the year and it was mentioned that your child researched a similar topic last year.</li><li>No matter what is introduced and/or studied, your child repeatedly revisits the same subject/topic/ideas.</li><li>Tasks are often completed with great attention to detail and/or intricate ideas/complexity.</li><li>You child demonstrates creativity of thought in the area(s) of _____.</li><li>Behaviors demonstrated often include _____.</li><li>Your child seems to quickly learn/recall factual information.</li><li>Your child seems to master basic skills quickly.</li><li>Your child possesses a vast amount of information.</li><li>There seems to be a sincere enjoyment in learning in your child.</li><li>In comparison to other children, your child seems to have an advanced vocabulary.</li></ul>

Social/Emotional
<ul><li>In relation to other students the same age, your child demonstrates great confidence in his or her ability to _____.</li><li>Depending on the situation, it's been observed that self-confidence is both present and absent. For example, when performing with the band or working independently, self-confidence soars. However, when assigned to cooperative learning groups, your child becomes more reserved.</li><li>When working with other students, your child often takes charge and/or assumes the leadership role.</li><li>Sometimes your child has difficulty realizing that other group members may have some good ideas and/or be able to contribute to the efforts of the group.</li><li>Your child has very high expectations for him- or herself.</li><li>It has been witnessed that your child is not shy about questioning already established rules and/or procedures.</li><li>When placed in new situations, your child seems to easily adapt.</li><li>Sometimes your child becomes very frustrated if it is time to submit an assignment and he or she hasn't completed it to his or her satisfaction.</li></ul>

Study Skills
<ul><li>You child seems to plan and manage his or her time effectively.</li><li>Your child responds positively when given checkpoints throughout a project.</li><li>Your child's planner is always completed and assignments are completed in a timely fashion.</li><li>During independent work time, your child often gets sidetracked and prefers to explore his or her own personal areas of interest.</li><li>Motivation is seen with topics of personal interest, but not those that are not deemed boring or unimportant.</li><li>Your child has a high tolerance for ambiguity.</li><li>Your child is noticeably resourceful and can improvise if needed.</li><li>Your child often wants to improve the quality of the work he or she is doing.</li><li>Task commitment is evident and intense.</li><li>Your child often talks about setting goals and accomplishes them.</li><li>Your child is highly productive.</li></ul>

Table 7.3,continued

Information Gathering
• Your child seems to demonstrate a sincere interest in learning.
• The above-mentioned sincerity is a bit more evident in some core areas.
• Basic, factual information seems to be learned rather quickly in comparison to other children.
• Often, the information your child learns is retained very quickly.
• Your child demonstrates great insight about topics and/or adult issues/world events.
• The vocabulary used to express ideas is often advanced and specific to the topic/subject being discussed.
• Your child is inquisitive in nature and asks questions that often connect different ideas/ views.
• Reading is your child's activity of choice during free time.
• Your child often seeks out those that share similar ideas and/or interests.
• I often notice your child talking with adults or older students.

understanding of the gifted behaviors demonstrated by their children while at school.

As positive, trusting relationships between the school and home are fostered over time, the value and support for the local gifted program will solidify. Program and communication consistency will add much creditability to the input provided by families to educators. The end result will be a gifted and talented program designed specifically for gifted CLD students, where sustained, consistent services that directly benefit the community in which the CLD families live can be individually provided.

Community

The final stakeholder crucial to the sustainability of quality gifted services is the community. NAGC Programming Standard 5.3.1 states, "Educators regularly engage families and community members for planning, programming, evaluating, and advocating." The term "regularly" intentionally sets the standard for consistency and defines the level of engagement. A consistent level of engagement occurs on a regular basis, not just when the program needs money or as a one-time support initiative. Parents and community members who are engaged on a regular basis are vital partners to the school organization.

In order for gifted CLD students to sincerely pursue their area of giftedness, there must be real-world outlets for them to explore and investigate their area of passion. Community partnerships are an effective way to offer gifted CLD students such opportunities. When the educators and the community partner in education, resources can be combined to offer students professional mentorship and/or relevant, real-world opportunities to explore their area of giftedness. As students navigate the school environment of high-stakes testing, coupled with college and career readiness, helping them discover their interest and aptitudes is vital in sustaining motivation in school. NAGC Programming Standard 5.7 elaborates the importance of identifying future career goals through facilitating mentorships, internships, and vocational programming experiences that align with the student's articulated interest and aptitudes. At this point, serving the gifted CLD student is no longer about teaching core curriculum content, but about helping the student become a contributing member of the community by actually putting knowledge into practice. As community partners witness the advantages of teaming up with local educators to assist gifted CLD students in the pursuit of their passions, the established trust and effective communication among the stakeholders remains foundational to the quality of the gifted program.

As represented in Figure 7.1, acknowledging the interplay between the school, home, and community is vital in designing a program model that best serves the gifted population on every campus and at every grade level.

Conclusion

The importance of such positive interplay when providing an authentic continuum of services to gifted CLD children cannot be overstated. From elementary school to middle school and on to high school, identification practices and quality gifted services are dependent on the effective communication and trust established between these three distinct entities. Parental responses to provided question stems help the teacher to observe behaviors and purposefully orchestrate experiences that develop gifted and talented behaviors, which lead to qualification for much deserved gifted services. When parents understand the gifted and talented program and how identification can lead to individualized educational opportunities for their child, the community in which the CLD student lives is also influenced. Community partnerships extend learning beyond the school walls and bring together valuable educational resources that benefit all stakeholders. The ability to foster positive interplay and create authentic ownership of the gifted services is the key to gifted programming longevity and success.

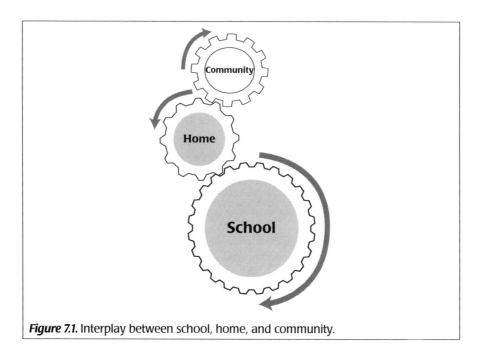

Figure 7.1. Interplay between school, home, and community.

Chapter 8

Program Evaluation

The purpose of Chapter 8 is to provide a rubric for evaluating the components of a gifted education program that serves a culturally and linguistically diverse student population. Relating this information to previous chapters will provide evaluative insights into effective interplay of program components.

Preview of Term(s):
- ⟡ *Qualitative*: A means to measure the quality of an activity by taking into consideration anecdotal information and nontraditional sources.
- ⟡ *Quantitative*: A means to statistically measure an activity.
- ⟡ *Embedded engagement*: Integrated activity that is authentic in nature, sustained over a period of time, and measured in progress.

Introduction

Performance and accountability are the cornerstones for ensuring program efficacy. Without the ability to evaluate, antiquated practices and ineffective work—*however best intentioned*—will continue. With the rapid growth of the CLD student population, responding quickly to student needs has never been more critical. Determining program performance success and responding effectively to accountability measures makes the need to evaluate program services even more imperative. Combining qualitative and quantitative measures to ensure comprehensive program evaluation allows for adjustment, selective abandonment, and growth, thus resulting in improved services to students.

> The use of multiple measures to determine program effectiveness and efficacy is vital.

One measure of program evaluation is a qualitative rubric. Table 8.1 extrapolates key components from each preceding chapter and applies the key components to evaluation. Where CLD student populations are present, the key components are found in gifted programs. The range of the rubric (minimal to complete) reflects the degree to which the component is present in the gifted program. A gifted education program may achieve different levels on different key components. Additionally, a component may be rated *complete* yet may not have matured into demonstrating a level of *exemplary*, which can be extended to consider programmatic evidence of exemplary status. The programmatic goal is to achieve or make progress in achieving the level of complete, replete with evidence of exemplary (complete +) as demonstrated in Figure 8.1.

Conclusion

Program evaluation is continuous and constant. Once the goal of exemplary is achieved, comprehensive program evaluation reinforces continued forward thinking. Constantly challenging the status quo is a premise of effective program evaluation. What serves a gifted program well historically will not necessarily be a hallmark of exemplary programming in the future. As the student population is ever changing, so must the programs that serve our students. Never before has the need for effective program evaluation been so critical. In order to create responsive gifted programming, current services and programming must be scrutinized and changed in order to affect exemplary services for our most promising students.

Table 8.1

Qualitative Rubric for Program Evaluation of CLD Components in Gifted Education Services

Chapter	Key Components	Minimal (Few)	Adequate (Most)	Complete (All)	Evidence of Exemplary (Complete +)
1	Program personnel possess a deep understanding and working knowledge of second language acquisition principles.				Certified in ESL. Trained in sheltered instruction.
2	Program personnel are keenly aware of the demographic changes impacting the school environment.				CLD representation in personnel. Program personnel are stakeholders in the community.
2	Program personnel are knowledgeable of a variety of assessment instruments for gifted education.				Personnel maintain professional updates in assessment. Demonstrated proficiency in implementing various types of assessment (culturally and linguistically responsive).
3	Program personnel are knowledgeable of accurate methodologies for assessing the educational system to accurately identify underrepresented student populations in gifted education.				All ethnicities are fully represented based on the percentages of student ethnicities. A variety of culturally and linguistically responsive instruments and methodologies are used to evaluate potential giftedness.
4	Gifted education program personnel are knowledgeable about other student special programs services (e.g., special education, literacy programs).				Personnel representing various special program services are integrated (as appropriate) into the gifted program service process.
4	Program personnel integrate gifted services with other special programs serving students.				Evidence of blending/integrating program services includes (but is not limited to) collaborative planning, co-teaching, and professional learning communities.
4	Representation from across student populations and special program groups is presented.				All special programs are fully represented based on the percentages of student qualification (as appropriate).
5	Authentic work is present and displayed throughout the school environment.				Evidence of student work is pervasive throughout the school and demonstrates best practice instruction and student metacognition.
5	Curriculum and instructional best practices work in concert to assure a culturally responsive environment that includes opportunities for meaningful learning.				Evidence of differentiated learning is present (every student's work is unique).

Table 8.1., continued

Chapter	Key Components	Minimal (Few)	Adequate (Most)	Complete (All)	Evidence of Exemplary (Complete +)
6	Program personnel are engaged in goal-oriented professional development.				There is an overall framework/structure (4P or other) that provides direction and is goal oriented for educators working with gifted CLD students.
6	Program personnel are engaged in professional collaboration activities (both formally and informally).				There is a predictable frequency of occurrence of activities that demonstrate professional collaboration on the part of the gifted educators and others who provide services to gifted CLD students.
6	Program administrators are engaged and proficient in supporting professional development.				Program administrators possess the necessary competencies to engage in higher order consultation, guidance, and leadership for gifted services.
7	Parents are integrated and engaged in the program.				There are orchestrated activities that incorporate parents on a consistent, authentic, and regular basis.
7	Community members are incorporated into the program services through embedded engagement.				There are embedded activities that incorporate community members on a consistent, authentic, and regular basis.
8	Program services are regularly reviewed and evaluated for demonstrated progress to exemplary level.				A variety of measures are used to determine program progress and success.

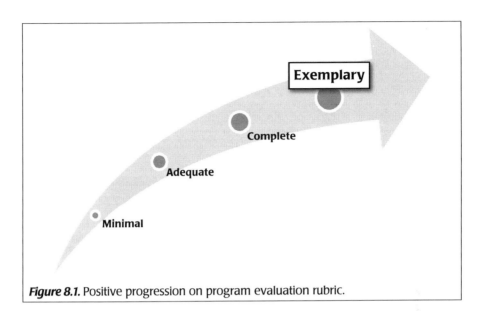

Figure 8.1. Positive progression on program evaluation rubric.

Conclusion

> At first people refuse to believe that a strange new thing can be done, then they begin to hope it can be done, then they see it can be done—then it is done and all the world wonders why it was not done centuries ago.
>
> —Frances H. Burnett

Within the chapters of this book are the authors' thoughts, beliefs, and vision for building collaboration coupled with the instructional and programmatic frameworks for serving gifted culturally and linguistically diverse students. The belief that educators will rally around an idea that something "new can be done" provides the hope that "it can be done." This book was written with the express hope that upon reading, educators see what can be done in their own schools.

With the conclusion of this book, we wonder why many of the practices and frameworks put forth in our writing were not done centuries ago. The greatest resources that educators have for doing "a strange new thing" lie within the existing systems; what is missing is the belief and the hope that it can be done—that the system can change. We believe that creating a new reality for identifying and serving culturally and linguistically diverse gifted students gives hope for change.

References

Beck, I. L., & McKeown, M. G. (1991). Conditions of vocabulary acquisition. In R. Barr, M. Kamil, P. Mosenthal, & P. D. Pearson (Eds.), *Handbook of reading research* (Vol. 2, pp. 789–814). New York, NY: Longman.

Betts, G. (1985). *The Autonomous Learner Model for the Gifted and Talented.* Greeley, CO: Autonomous Learning Publications and Specialists.

Calderón, M. (2007). *Teaching reading to English language learners, grades 6–12.* Thousand Oaks, CA: Corwin Press.

Cohen, J., McAlister, K., Rolstad, K., & MacSwan, J. (2005). *Proceedings of the 4th International Symposium on Bilingualism.* Somerville, MA: Cascadilla Press.

Collier, V. P., & Thomas, W. P. (2004). The astounding effectiveness of dual language education for all. *NABE Journal of Research and Practice, 2(1),* 1–20.

Collier, V. P., & Thomas, W. P. (2007). Predicting second language academic success in English using the Prism Model. In J. Cummins & C. Davison (Eds.), *International handbook of English language teaching, Part 1* (pp. 333–348). New York, NY: Springer.

Collier, V. P., & Thomas, W. P. (2009). *Educating English learners for a transformed world.* Albuquerque, NM: Fuente Press.

Cummins, J. (1979). Linguistic interdependence and the educational development of bilingual children. *Review of Educational Research, 49,* 222–251.

Cummins, J. (1981). The role of primary language development in promoting educational success for language minority students. In California State Department of Education (Ed.), *Schooling and language minority students: A theoretical framework* (pp. 3–49). Los Angeles, CA: National Dissemination and Assessment Center.

Cummins, J. (n.d.). *Bilingual children's mother tongue: Why is it important for education?* Retrieved from http://www.iteachilearn.org/cummins/mother.htm

Fountas, I. C., & Pinnell, G. S. (1996). *Guided reading: Good first teaching for all children.* Portsmouth, NH: Heinemann.

Frayer, D., Frederick, W. C., & Klausmeier, H. J. (1969). *A schema for testing the level of cognitive mastery.* Madison, WI: Wisconsin Center for Education Research.

Hollingworth, L. S. (1926). *Gifted children: Their nature and nurture.* New York, NY: Macmillan.

Hollingsworth, L. S. (1936). The development of personality in highly intelligent children. *National Elementary School Principal, 15,* 272–281.

Imbeau, M. B. (2006). Designing a professional development plan. In J. H. Purcell & R. D. Eckert (Eds.), *Designing services and programs for high-ability learners: A guidebook for gifted education* (pp. 184–194). Thousand Oaks, CA: Corwin Press.

Isaksen, S. G., & Treffinger, D. J. (1985). *Creative Problem Solving: The basic course.* Buffalo, NY: Bearly Limited.

Isurin, L. (2005). *Cross linguistic transfer in word order: Evidence from L1 forgetting and L2 acquisition.* Retrieved from http://www.lingref.com/isb/4/086ISB4.PDF

Kagan, S. (1994). *Cooperative learning.* San Clemente, CA: Kagan Publishing.

Kaplan, S. (1997). *Facilitating the understanding of depth and complexity.* Retrieved from http://www.texaspsp.org/all/DepthComplexity.pdf

Krashen, S. (1982). *Principles and practices in second language acquisition.* Oxford, England: Pergamon Press.

Krashen, S. D., & Terrell, T. D. (1983). *The natural approach: Language acquisition in the classroom.* Oxford, England: Pergamon Press.

Lafferty, S. M. (n.d.). *Meeting the needs of the academically gifted.* Retrieved from http://go.hrw.com/resources/go_sc/gen/HSTPR078.PDF

Landrum, M. S., Callahan, C. M., & Shaklee, B. D. (2001). *Aiming for excellence: Gifted program standards: Annotations to the NAGC Pre-K-Grade 12 Gifted Program Standards.* Waco, TX: Prufrock Press.

Marland, S. P., Jr. (1972). *Education of the gifted and talented: Report to the Congress of the United States by the U.S. Commissioner of Education and background papers submitted to the U.S. Office of Education,* 2 vols. Washington, DC: U.S. Government Printing Office. (Government Documents, Y4.L 11/2: G36)

Marzano, R., & Pickering, D. (2005). *Building academic vocabulary teacher's manual.* Alexandria, VA: Association of Supervision and Curriculum Development.

National Association for Gifted Children. (2010). *NAGC pre-K–grade 12 gifted programming standards: A blueprint for quality gifted education programs.* Washington, DC: Author.

Okagaki, L., & Sternberg, R. J. (1993). Parental beliefs and children's early school performance. *Child Development, 64*(1), 36–56.

Renzulli, J. S. (1979). What makes giftedness? Reexamining a definition. *Phi Delta Kappan, 60,* 180–184.

Renzulli, J. S. (1986). The three-ring conception of giftedness: A developmental model for promoting creativity. In R. J. Sternberg & J. Davidson (Eds.), *Conceptions of giftedness* (pp. 246–279). New York, NY: Cambridge University Press.

Richert, S. (1985). Identification of gifted students: An update. *Roeper Review, 8,* 68–72.

Silverman, L. K. (1997). The construct of asynchronous development. *Peabody Journal of Education, 72*(3/4), 36–58.

Slocumb, P. D. (with Olenchak, F. R.). (2006). *Equity in gifted education: A state initiative.* Austin, TX: Texas Education Agency.

Tabors, P. (2008). *One child, two languages: A guide for early childhood educators of children learning English as a second language* (2nd ed.). Baltimore, MD: Paul H. Brookes.

Thomas, W. P., & Collier, V. P. (2001). *A national study of school effectiveness for language minority students' long-term academic achievement.* Retrieved from http://crede.berkeley.edu/research/llaa/1.1pdfs/1.1_16_conclusions.pdf

Tomlinson, C. A. (1995). *Differentiating instruction for advanced learners in the mixed-ability middle school classroom.* Retrieved from http://www.kidsource.com/kidsource/content/diff_instruction.html

Tomlinson, C. A. (1999). *The differentiated classroom: Responding to the needs of all learners.* Alexandria, VA: Association of Supervision and Curriculum Development.

U.S. Census Bureau. (2007). *American community survey.* Retrieved from http://www.census.gov/acs

VanTassel-Baska, J. (1986). Effective curriculum and instructional models for talented students. *Gifted Child Quarterly, 30,* 164–169.

VanTassel-Baska, J. (1995). The development of talent through curriculum. *Roeper Review, 18,* 98–102.

VanTassel-Baska, J., & Stambaugh, T. (2006). *Comprehensive curriculum for gifted learners* (3rd ed.). Boston, MA: Allyn & Bacon.

Vogt, M., & Echevarria, J. (2008). *99 ideas and activities for teaching English learners with the SIOP® model*. Boston, MA: Allyn & Bacon.

Vygotsky, L. S. (1962). *Thought and language.* Cambridge, MA: The MIT Press.

Wenger, W., & Poe, R. (1996) *The Einstein factor: A proven new method for increasing your intelligence.* Rocklin, CA: Prima Pub.

About the Authors

Lezley Collier Lewis is an educational consultant, author, and statewide expert on second language acquisition. Dr. Lewis received a Doctorate of Educational Administration from Texas A&M University and a Doctorate of Jurisprudence from Texas Tech School of Law. She has been instrumental in developing, instituting, and sustaining innovative educational programs focused on English language learner (ELL) success. Dr. Lewis developed one of the first two-way, dual language programs instituted in Texas in the early 1990s and continues to work with school districts to streamline resources in order to create and sustain successful ELL programs.

With more than 20 years in education, Dr. Lewis has worked in a variety of capacities in both the public and private sectors. She has served as a strategist for school districts implementing systemic change through strategic planning. Her teaching background includes P–16, bilingual/ESL education, secondary world language, and public school district-level administration. However, her greatest accomplishment is that of being a parent of a public school teacher.

Annie Rivera is an educational consultant in bilingual and ESL instruction, professional development, and program development for rural, suburban, and urban school districts and campuses. Her teaching background includes transitional bilingual, dual language, ESL, and regular education classroom instruction at the elementary and secondary levels in both private and public schools in Texas and abroad, as well as at the college level. In addition, Rivera has also served as instructional specialist and district-level coordinator for bilingual/

ESL programs. Proud of her Korean heritage, native-Texan roots, and families in Latin America, Rivera describes herself as being both trilingual, triliterate, and tricultural. She is also a product of a gifted program, foreign language in the elementary school (FLES) program, and heritage language school. This identity and personal experiences not only give her unique perspective and insights into serving CLD students and meeting their needs, but it also instills in her a deep-rooted passion for advocating multilingualism in all students. Rivera is an Ivy League graduate from the University of Pennsylvania and plans to pursue her doctorate in the area of international education. Rivera resides in the Dallas area with a very supportive extended family, especially Greg and Theresa Jeong; her loving husband, Gonzalo; and her beautiful daughter, Camila.

Debbie Roby, a graduate of The Ohio State University ('92 B.S., '97 M.Ed.), has been an educator/administrator in the Ohio, North Carolina, and Texas public school systems. Debbie is currently the Supervisor of Gifted Education in Lewisville, TX. Throughout her career, Debbie has had the privilege of providing instructional support and leadership to dedicated administrators and teachers who deliver quality educational services to students. Debbie has extensive experience writing both elementary and secondary curriculum for the gifted learner. She is passionate about identifying and serving frequently overlooked gifted children, many of whom are culturally and linguistically diverse. In addition, Debbie has facilitated extensive professional development sessions that address the advantages of authentic work, best practice instruction that leads to the production of authentic work, and classroom implications of its use. While spending the last two decades working as a professional educator, Debbie and her husband, Aaron, have been proudly raising two very active boys, Adam and Mark.